The ENCYCLOPEDIA OF PRINTMAKING TECHNIQUES

THE
ENCYCLOPEDIA
OF
PRINTMAKING
TECHNIQUES

Judy Martin

RUNNING PRESS
PHILADELPHIA · LONDON

A QUARTO BOOK

9 8 7 6 5 4 3 2 1
Digit on the right indicates the number of this printing

ISBN 0-7624-0258-X

Library of Congress Cataloging-in-Publication Number
97-68281

This book was designed and produced by
Quarto Publishing plc
The Old Brewery
6 Blundell Street
London N7 9BH

Senior editor Kate Kirby
Editor Hazel Harrison
Senior art editor Amanda Bakhiar
Designer Nick Clark
Picture Researcher Liz Eddison
Photographers Duncan Phillips, Chas Wilder, Les Weis
Art Director Moira Clinch
Publishing Director Janet Slingsby

The author would like to thank the artists who have
contributed work to this book, particularly the members of
North Star Studios, Brighton, who provided technical
demonstrations. Special thanks also to Kate Kirby for
efficient and good-humoured editorial support on this and
previous projects.

Publishers note

Working with printmaking chemicals demands care, as
some you will be using are poisonous and/or corrosive.
This means you must take precautions; always follow the
manufacturer's instructions; always store chemicals
securely in clearly marked non-food containers, and keep
them well out of reach of children. As far as the techniques
used to apply the chemicals, and the effects they produce
are concerned, all statements, information, and advice
given here are beiweved to be true and accurate. However,
neither the author, copyright holder, or pubisher can
accept any legal liability for errors or omissions.

Typeset by Bookworm Typesetting, Manchester
Manufactured in Hong Kong by Regent Publishing
Services Ltd.
Printed in China by Leefung Asco Printers Ltd.

This book may be ordered by mail from the
publisher. Please include $2.50 for postage
and handling. *But try your bookstore first!*

Running Press Book Publishers
125 South Twenty-second Street
Philadelphia, Pennsylvania 19103 4399

INTRODUCTION

✳

Printmaking covers an impressively wide range of activities and pictorial matter – there is something for everyone here. But printmaking studios, with their strange, alchemical combinations of unfamiliar materials, purpose-made tools and monumental machinery, can seem like alien territory, even to experienced artists quite comfortable with other kinds of studio practice.

However, there is no need to be daunted by the technicalities, because many of the printmaking processes are very straightforward and easy to grasp. Some, such as lithography and etching, are inherently more complex, but they can be learned in stages so that the newcomer can gradually build confidence and grow in ambition. In fact, the necessity to follow specific technical procedures provides a framework for the creative side of image-making that many artists regard as a supportive element. As you become immersed in practicalities, the process itself suggests ways of interpreting your image.

This book is an invaluable introduction to printmaking methods, taking you step by step through the technical details as well as providing inspirational examples of prints in all media. Although

some of the print processes have a long tradition and are carried out in much the same ways as they always were, there can be no doubt that modern technology has made it easier to extend the potential of individual printmaking methods and to combine their effects in multimedia images.

Well-known professional artists who produce "edition" prints often have much of the processing carried out for them by equally professional print technicians, but in this book the priority is to relate the techniques and inspirational images to things you can easily achieve yourself with readily available equipment and facilities. Although it is necessary to have access to a properly equipped studio and presses in order to develop the full potential of most techniques, there are methods you can carry out from start to finish working on your kitchen or family-room table. Keep this in mind as you look through the book and choose the printmaking areas you might like to work with. Once you have understood the principles and mastered some basic techniques, you can bring your own inventiveness and creativity into play to adapt the chosen methods to suit your style of work and situation.

Contents

TECHNIQUES

❋

THE STEP-BY-STEP DEMONSTRATIONS IN THIS SECTION OF THE BOOK ARE THE IDEAL INTRODUCTION TO THE RANGE OF PRINTMAKING METHODS. THE SEQUENCES ARE DESIGNED TO PROVIDE A CLEAR EXPLANATION OF WHAT THE MATERIALS, TOOLS, AND EQUIPMENT CAN DO IN EACH CASE, AND WHY CERTAIN PROCEDURES ARE NECESSARY. ONCE YOU BEGIN TO WORK WITH YOUR CHOSEN METHOD, YOU WILL SOON ACQUIRE THE PRACTICAL KNOWLEDGE THAT ENABLES YOU TO THINK CREATIVELY IN TERMS.OF PRINTMAKING ITSELF.

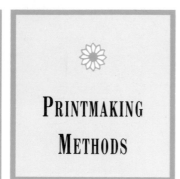

PRINTMAKING METHODS

There are two main reasons for choosing to produce an original image as a print, one being to obtain a number of identical copies. The motive for this may be to originate pictures as multiple images or to reinterpret an existing painting or drawing in print form. Because prints sell more cheaply than unique objects, they are accessible to people who do not normally invest in art and can thus represent a useful share of an artist's income. For the amateur, there is a considerable pleasure in having works on paper that can be sold cheaply or given to friends, while one or more can be retained by the artist.

The second reason for making prints is that each process produces characteristic visual qualities quite different from those of a directly drawn or painted image. For example, the flat, glossy color areas you see in a linocut or silkscreen print cannot easily be obtained with paint and brush; and the grainy, integrated textures of chalk drawing and ink washes produced by lithography are distinctly different in feel to similar marks applied directly on paper. Etching is a law unto itself: an etched line is not at all like a drawn line, and there are many ways of achieving etched textures that give an exciting variety to this long-established medium.

The way the image is produced influences not only the character of the finished work, but the way you conceive and plan it. Before you start to consider which processes would suit you best, take account of the following basic principles.

Basic principles

The methods of producing a printed image can be divided into four main categories: relief printing, intaglio, plano-graphic (printing from a flat surface) as in lithography, and stencil processes as applied in screenprinting. In the relief-printing techniques of linocut, woodcut, and wood engraving (pages 36–53), the original flat surface of the wood or linoleum block represents the printing surface. Any parts of the design not to be printed are cut away, leaving the image raised in relief. This is inked, usually with a roller, and transferred to paper by direct pressure.

Intaglio processes – drypoint, mezzotint, and etching – are the exact opposite. All these are usually done on metal plates, and the design is incised or etched into the surface. It is the sunken lines and areas of the plate that are printed, by pushing ink into them and applying heavy pressure to press the paper into the inked marks; the original surface level of an intaglio plate represents the white in a black-and-white image.

Lithography is a planographic process, meaning that the printing and non-printing areas are on the same level. The image is drawn on a metal plate (or litho stone) and processed so that it "sets" into the grain of the surface. Lithographic prints can be taken by direct pressure or by offsetting. On an offset press, plate and paper are placed side by side; a roller travels over the plate and picks up the inked image; traveling back, it deposits the image.

Screenprinting is basically a stenciling process. The screen has a stretched, fine mesh which transmits an even layer

Elisabeth Harden
Oriental Poppies (lithograph)
In lithography, the artist's drawing and painting skills are directly applied to developing the image on the plate, using inks and crayons. This can result in a very vivid, spontaneous feel to the finished print, although the buildup of colors has to be carefully planned, with each individual hue printed from a separate plate, and mixed colors achieved by overprinting. The marks made by the drawing materials supply the varied surface qualities of the image, but the grain of the litho plate also influences texture.

of ink under pressure. To create the image, parts of the mesh must be blocked so that they do not allow the ink through. There are many different ways of preparing stencils, all of which produce characteristically different qualities in the imagery.

Negative and positive

A printed image taken by direct pressure is always reversed on the paper because the original block or plate is in face-to-face contact with it. Relief and intaglio processes both produce reversed images, as does lithographic printing on a direct-pressure press. In offset lithography, the image is not reversed, because it is put down on the paper in the same position as it was picked up from the plate – an intermediary surface carries the inked image, and there is no direct contact between plate and paper. In screenprinting, too, the image is "right-reading," because the ink passes through the screen mesh rather than being printed from it.

Jonathan Heale
Tree (woodcut)
The relief printing technique of woodcut and linocut produces strong, highly graphic effects, which show most clearly in a powerful monochrome image like this. The stark black-and-white contrast requires the artist to select essential details from the subject and organize a balance of tones.

Moira Wills
Green Room (screenprint)
Bold shapes and clear colors are frequently the hallmark of screenprints made from hand-cut stencils, although there are many ways to vary the qualities of surface texture. Here the artist uses a lot of lively pattern detail to keep the eye moving around the image.

Screenprinting inks provide a wide range of colors that have great brilliance and luminosity, but can be mixed or overprinted to produce deep, rich tones and muted hues.

This left-to-right reversal is not the only "opposite" element you have to keep in mind when preparing images for printing. Often you are required to work in negative – that is, the marks you make with your printmaking tools represent the non-printing areas of the design. In relief prints, the parts of the block that you actively cut away surround the parts that will be seen as the image. In screenprinting, where you are preparing a stencil to print, for example, blue areas of the image, the stencil itself will consist of all those areas that will not be blue. Conversely, in lithography and most intaglio processes, the marks you make are those that directly create the image, as in drawing or painting.

These concepts can seem confusing when put into words; they start to make sense as you begin to put them into practice. There are also exceptions to the rules – resist techniques for preparing a screen image, for example, and one or two specific etching techniques, when you do invert the normal procedures. For this reason, you need to start with any printmaking method, simply learning the basics that give you the ability to think through the process in logical steps. As you gain experience and confidence, you can discover the variations that enable you to exploit the properties of your medium more fully and apply them to an expressive rendering of your subject.

Collage print

Color and texture

Prints of the same subject carried out in the full range of media show some of the characteristic differences between printmaking processes and their effects. Monoprints and collage prints are technically quite simple to make, but can provide a wide variety of painterly qualities. The intaglio methods of drypoint and mezzotint are primarily tonal, but differently approached – drypoint by drawing positively in black line and tone, mezzotint by burnishing whites out of dark texture. Similarly, wood engraving typically appears as white lines on black, while the other relief methods – woodcut and linocut – more often rely on black key-line images, although both are easily adapted to color printing. Etching, lithography, and screenprinting each incorporate a variety of techniques, allowing equally varied, simple, or sophisticated surface effects.

Etching

Mezzotint

Wood engraving

Monoprint

Woodcut

Drypoint

Linocut

Lithography

Screenprint

THE WORK ENVIRONMENT

There is no doubt that the ideal situation for learning and practicing all the major printmaking processes is a properly equipped print studio. For most non-professional artists, the easiest and least expensive way to achieve this goal is to join organized classes in printmaking at a local art school or adult-education institute. For the more ambitious who would like to devote some regular time to specific processes, it may be possible to rent time in a professional studio or join a co-operative of artists sharing printmaking facilities.

However, having no access, or very limited access, to a studio by no means disqualifies you from producing interesting prints. Monoprints, linocuts, woodcuts, wood engravings, and collage prints can all be prepared and printed at home. The main advantage of using a print studio is access to a printing press, which enables you to produce reliable, good-quality impressions quite quickly. But you can produce finished prints from flat surfaces and blocks by a simple hand-printing method. Alternatively, you can prepare printing blocks at home and make hand-printed proofs, then arrange to use a print studio only for the time you need to refine the design and take your final prints on the press.

Printing presses

There are various printing presses, some dedicated to one printing method, others adaptable to more than one. A relief-printing press typically relies on direct pressure. In flat-bed presses such as the Albion and Columbian types, the block is placed on the bed of the press and an upper surface is brought down to exert heavy pressure on paper and block. An alternative is the old-style type-proofing press, formerly used by typesetters. This kind of press has a sunken bed in which a thick wood or wood-mounted linoleum block can be set. A cylinder with the paper attached is rolled across the block under pressure.

Intaglio printing is done on a roller press, a flat, heavy metal bed suspended between two rollers. The space between the rollers is adjusted to vary the pressure as required; the metal intaglio plate with paper laid on top is positioned on the bed, and the bed is passed between the rollers. This press can be adapted to relief printing, provided that the original block is not too thick to be accommodated by the rollers. A relief-printing press, however, cannot normally be used for intaglio because it does not exert sufficient pressure to force the paper down into the sunken areas of the plate.

For offset lithography, a specialized press is required. This has a long bed on which the paper and plate are

positioned side by side. A very large, heavy roller occupying the whole width of the bed trundles along its entire length, moved either by a handle or an electrically powered mechanism. The rubber "blanket" around the roller picks up ink from the plate as it passes forward, then puts it down on the paper as it moves back.

Large printing presses are cumbersome, heavy, and extremely expensive. Even if you could find an affordable

Using a flat-bed press
1 The upright section of the press supports a heavy platen that moves downward when the bar is pulled across. The flat bed is rolled out from underneath to position block and paper, then taken back underneath before pressure is applied.

Proofing press
This kind of press was originally designed for printing type blocks to produce galley proofs of texts. The bed of the press accommodates the height of the type blocks, so is ideal for printing woodcut blocks and wood-mounted linoleum. The paper is fitted on the cylinder, which is then rolled over the inked block.

Etching press
A press for printing intaglio plates, which are only a fraction of an inch thick. When a geared handle is turned, a flat metal bed passes between two heavy metal rollers. To soften and spread the pressure, blankets are used to cushion the action of the rollers.

2 The handle is turned the other way to take the bed right back underneath the platen, to position the block centrally so that even pressure will be applied.

3 With the bed in position, the artist grasps the bar and pulls it toward him, which lowers the platen onto the bed. This takes some effort, as the downward pressure activated by the movement of the bar is powerful.

secondhand one, you might need to have the floor of your workroom strengthened before the press could be installed. New roller-press models are more compact and lightweight. The capital outlay is considerable, but you will have a machine that will last for years. On a smaller scale, tabletop versions of the intaglio roller press are available at reasonable prices.

Screenprinting facilities
You can easily set up a small-scale screenprinting operation at home, since the basic equipment is self-contained, relatively lightweight, and can be constructed to a required size. You must have a perfectly

flat surface for printing, so it is best to hinge the screen to a permanent printing bed or base board so it can be raised and lowered freely. Screens can be bought readymade from some art and craft retailers, or you can make your own – there are several specialist publications that explain this in full detail.

If you are working in a print studio, you may be using a metal printing frame attached to a vacuum bed. The frame is adjustable so that the screen can be securely locked into it. The printing bed has a network of small holes across its full length and width. When the mechanism that creates the vacuum is switched on during

Metal drying racks
The metal frames form a stack, each frame hinged at the back so it can be lifted easily to slip in prints on lower layers. This kind of drying rack is highly suitable for relief prints, screenprints, and lithographs.

Ceiling racks
1 These custom-built wooden racks have slots containing a ball-and-wire mechanism that grips the top edge of the print and allows the paper to hang straight.

2 To insert the print, the ball is pushed upward and the paper slipped in against the wire. When the ball drops back, its own weight secures the paper. The same action releases the print.

Safety features
The acid bath in an etching studio is one of the most obviously hazardous work areas and needs special facilities. This one is below a ventilator hood and can be completely enclosed by pulling down the plastic sides of the boxed-in area. The artist takes the precaution of using goggles and rubber gloves when working with the acid.

printing, it creates suction from below that holds the paper down on the flat surface.

Work areas
The other advantage of a properly set-up studio is that there is an allotted space for each stage of the work. This helps to keep the work clean and the tools and equipment in good condition. Also, different chemicals and materials can be stored separately to avoid accident or contamination.

If you are working at home on relief prints or screenprinting, there are a few basic guidelines to take into account. For simple, practical reasons, it is helpful to have separate areas for preparation and printing, because this allows you to work on both at one session without taking time to clear up and reorganize. For example, cutting blocks or preparing a screen stencil could be done in

one area and printing from them in another. You can also keep sharp cutting tools away from other equipment.

One important space that it is easy to overlook is an area where prints can be left to dry. You may wish to print twenty or thirty impressions at one time, in which case you will have a lot of pieces of paper that have to be stored separately for up to two days – and left somewhere where they can dry flat with no risk of sticking together. A simple solution is a "washing-line" system of cords strung above eye level, on which prints can be hung using bulldog clips or similar fastenings. If you have flat files, which are useful storage for clean paper and drawings or paintings as well, you can lay out the prints for drying as the top layer of each drawer. Or you can construct a wood or metal shelving system with shallow openings so that the prints can be leafed in to lie flat on the shelves.

Studio drying systems include wooden ceiling-hung racks with ball-and-wire attachments that grip the top edge of the prints, and metal-frame stacks that flap up and down so you can insert the prints to lie flat on a wire grid in several layers. Intaglio prints, which are taken on damp paper, are usually pressed between boards while drying, so that the paper does not buckle. The prints are interleaved with blotting or tissue paper to prevent them from coming into contact with each other.

Safety
Safety factors are particularly important in both etching and lithography. Various stages of

etching involve working on the metal plates with heat, acid, or flammable substances, while chemical preparations are used in lithography, and the flexible metal plates and mechanical press need careful management. However, under proper guidance, both processes are quite safe. Any chemical that gives off fumes must be used in an area with good ventilation, and goggles, a face mask, and rubber gloves are necessary precautions when you are dealing with acid or other caustic liquids.

Generally, however, your alertness to the safety angle should be much the same as when you are cooking or carrying out home repairs. Don't leave things to "cook" on a hotplate; don't leave sharp tools out, or mix up different types of equipment; immediately clean up liquids or inks that spill on the floor so that you don't slip.

PRODUCING PRINTS

Getting from the picture in your mind's eye to the finished print on paper is not just a matter of technical skill, but also of working with the medium appropriately at each stage of processing. This includes the way you initially conceive and prepare your

image for print form. For the beginner, this is a chicken-and-egg situation – if you don't know what the process can do, how can you plan the final image? On the other hand, if you haven't begun with a definite visual idea, what are you to work on in order to learn how to print?

To find out what the particular marks and materials you apply will turn into when processed and printed, you can start off by working direct on a block, plate, or screen in a purely abstract manner. A test plate or block is not an unusual first step. You probably won't

From drawing to print
1 The composition of the still life is worked out in a detailed pencil and watercolor sketch. The artist needs to establish the overall shapes clearly and plot the color and tonal variations within them. These are to be translated into a three-color print – yellow, red, green – in which mixed hues will be achieved by overprinting.

achieve a finished image with much form to it this way, but you may find you have produced a useful reference chart for future use.

Working drawings
More commonly, you will start with some reference work – a sketch, drawing, painting, or photograph – as the basis for the print. The first thing to realize is that any form of printmaking is an interpretive, not a reproductive method. In other words, the print will not look exactly like the original. The working drawing is a guideline to composition,

visual qualities such as the relationship of line work and solid color areas, and the overall scheme of color. These elements have to be translated into the new medium and cannot be copied exactly, although in all media you can trace and transfer an image as your starting point – it is not necessary to redraw the composition from scratch.

For the inexperienced printmaker interested in producing prints in two or more colors, the working drawing is an essential step. You have to make a separate block, screen, or plate for each

2 Yellow is the dominant color, contributing to each aspect of the still life, so it covers a broad area of the first printing plate. However, it will not have this full-strength effect in the final print. Being light-toned, it will recede somewhat against the other colors.

main color, and figure out whether you can overprint colors to produce mixed hues. Sometimes, once you have isolated the areas for printing one color, you will find that an originally realistic image is reduced to a series of more or less abstract shapes, and you cannot relate this to the other colors without some initial guideline. It may be best to make a fairly detailed working drawing and trace each color element with some accuracy. As you learn more of your craft, you can cut down the detail of this preliminary stage and simplify your plan to the bare essentials.

Experienced printmakers may start immediately without doing this at all because they feel confident of working direct with the print medium and can anticipate how the stages will gradually pull together.

Proofing and printing

In order to understand how the image is translating into print, proofs are taken at various stages. These working proofs also act as guidelines for further stages, such as the continued cutting of a block or processing of a plate; until you have seen the image as it prints, you will not know where to develop it further or where to make corrections and adjustments.

On a relief block, you can take a rubbing rather than a printed proof, which is less laborious and gives you a fair idea of the image quality. An etching can be proofed at any stage, but on a mezzotint or drypoint plate the printing areas are relatively fragile – too many proofs cause the surface to deteriorate – so what you gain from proofing you may lose in the final printing.

When you are ready to take the final prints, you can run a whole edition. An edition is a numbered set of identical prints – in commercial terms, the numbering is a safeguard of their value, and professional artists' plates or blocks are cancelled after an edition has been completed. The artist chooses the number of prints in an edition; sometimes it may depend on how the printing surface stands up to wear, as with drypoint and mezzotint. An artist's proof is a finished print that does not form part of the edition set – the first few trials of the final printing may become artist's proofs if the quality is good.

3 The red obviously has to be strongest in the tomatoes and will print lightly over the yellow on the bowl in order to produce a warm orange. In the peppers, it is used tonally rather than as a distinct color, to create the subtle shadows that model the forms.

4 The green printing has a more linear character, defining the contours of the forms quite strongly. As with the red, the color has two functions, providing local color in the green pepper and enhancing the detail and modeling of the red and yellow fruits.

Elisabeth Harden
Peppers and Tomatoes
(lithograph)
The print is less heavily modeled than the original, since it contains no black that would correspond to the pencil drawing. The bright colors have a lush, fresh feeling appropriate to the subject. Dark shadows emerge from the overprinting of all three colors.

Inks and papers

The work done with the printmaking materials is not the only factor in the finished qualities of the print; the way you ink the image and the paper you print on contribute other surface values. At the later stages of preparing any kind of print, your proof stages should ideally use the same inking procedure and type of paper you intend for the finished version, as only then can you see the true effect.

Obviously different methods of printing require different properties from ink and paper, and brandname inks, available from specialist suppliers, are purpose-made for each one. Block-printing inks are more widely sold and can be bought in most good art-supply stores. In some cases – notably relief printing and screenprinting – you may find a choice between water-based or oil-based inks. Typically, oil-based types give the smoothest coverage and the most versatile effects, but the prints take longer to dry, and blocks or screens have to be cleaned up with the appropriate solvent. If in doubt, explain to the supplier what you intend to do and get advice on the right type and texture of ink and color choices available for your kind of work. If you are studio-based, the supervising technician or teacher can advise.

Most relief and screen prints can be made on almost any kind of paper – even on fabric – but the weight, thickness, and finish of the paper affects the appearance of the final image. Again, you may need to get advice on exactly what is needed in your case, but the following are some basic guidelines:

● For early proofing of block prints, screens, and lithographs, inexpensive newsprint or cartridge paper are quite adequate. Good-quality cartridge papers are also suitable for final proofs. Use a fairly substantial kind, as very thin papers may buckle under the ink.

● For processes which involve dampening the paper, mainly the intaglio processes, do not use anything too flimsy or open-textured, such as unsized papers which may disintegrate when wetted. However, papers that are too thick and stiff will not penetrate the intaglio and will pick up a broken impression. The best papers for intaglio are good-quality drawing and watercolor papers, which come in a variety of weights, thicknesses, and surface textures.

● Avoid extremes of surface texture – on exceptionally smooth, coated papers, ink can slide or smudge easily. You might, for example, get a double impression if the paper slips on a relief block during printing. Equally, be wary of very thick, heavily toothed papers, which may resist the ink.

● If you are interested in using decoratively colored or textured papers, bear in mind that they will contribute specific qualities to the finished print which may not integrate appropriately. However, lightly toned non-white papers – ivory or cream – and fibrous, lightweight Japanese papers are popular with printmakers. Strong base colors can be planned in as a specific element of an image; you can print white ink onto a colored surface if required.

Papers

Different kinds of papers have practical purposes in printmaking, as well as providing the base material for the finished print. In intaglio printing, blotting, and tissue papers (top, upper layers) are needed to prepare and store the dampened printing paper; prints can be taken on a variety of surfaces, including fine handmade or good-quality mold-made drawing and watercolor papers (above). Textured and colored papers (right) are useful for collage work and relief printing. To develop a printed image from an existing drawing or working study, you will also need tracing and transfer paper (below).

MONOPRINTS

A monoprint, as its name implies, is a unique impression made by applying printing ink to a flat surface and transferring it to paper. The method excludes one of the usual main purposes of printmaking, which is to obtain multiple copies of a single image, but the marks and textures obtained are characteristically different from those drawn or painted directly on paper. Monoprint is of particular interest to beginners in printmaking, because no presses or special studio equipment are needed.

Tools and materials

The printing surface can be anything which is flat, smooth, and non-absorbent. Suitable materials are a sheet of glass,

1

2

3

4

5

Monoprint equipment
1 Brushes; **2** papers; **3** glass mixing slab; **4** block-printing inks; **5** palette knife; **6** roller.

plastic, or metal; a slab of polished stone; or a section of plastic-faced wood or composition board. To create your image, you can apply block-printing inks (or oil paints) using any suitable implements – brushes, rollers, sticks, rags, sponges, or palette knives – to build up the design, just as though you were drawing or painting on paper. Then you simply lay a sheet of paper over it and rub firmly but evenly across the back of the paper. When you lift it, the

6

image is printed in reverse, as with relief printing methods.

Developing the print
Monoprints can be graphic monochrome studies or vigorous multicolored images. You can also overprint; for example, to build up thin color "glazes," develop dark tones, or lay in line work over solid-color areas. You do this by taking your first print, then cleaning the working surface and reworking with ink to take a second impression.

To overprint accurately, you need to use a simple form of registration. You can simply align the paper to the edges of the surface you are printing from; or if this is not large enough to give a good margin of paper around the printed image, you can lay a larger registration sheet beneath, visible on at least two sides, and align the printing paper to that. In the demonstration sequence shown here, the artist places a working sketch beneath the sheet of glass as a guide for each painting stage and for registration of overprintings.

Although you cannot produce a series of prints by re-inking, as you can with a etched plate or incised block, you can sometimes obtain two or three impressions from one inking; they will become gradually fainter, coarser-textured, and less colorful. There are various ways you can experiment with this medium, apart from the way you prepare the initial design. Variations in thickness of the ink and the pressure you apply to the back of the paper will affect both the tone and texture of the print.

Printing from glass
1 This method of preparing a monoprint image involves painting on the surface of the glass slab as you would on paper. The artist is using printing inks and has placed a rough sketch underneath the glass as a guide.

2 The print is pulled by laying paper on the glass and smoothing it down with your hand, a spoon, or a roller. This produces a typically softer, more textured impression than in the original painting.

2 By dragging and lifting the ink with a rag dampened with mineral spirits, she draws free, broad shapes in the color area.

3 The paper is placed over the glass sheet, aligned to the left-hand edge of the working drawing below the glass, and the print is pulled by hand-rubbing. This gives a soft, moody monochrome image.

Printing from acetate
If you work on acetate sheet rather than glass, you can take the print on a press rather than by hand. The additional pressure makes the colors stronger and the textures more detailed.

Overprinting
1 For the first stage of a three-stage print, the artist rolls out a flat layer of thin ink on glass. A sketch guide is positioned underneath the glass.

4 The second stage is prepared by painting on the glass with several colors. The underlying sketch is the guide for positioning the colors so they will overprint accurately on the monochrome image.

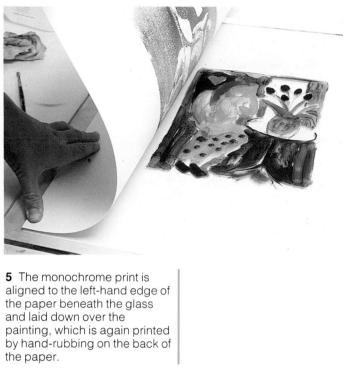

5 The monochrome print is aligned to the left-hand edge of the paper beneath the glass and laid down over the painting, which is again printed by hand-rubbing on the back of the paper.

6 The artist partially removes the painting by cleaning it off with mineral spirits on a rag. She then reworks the dark toned areas with fresh ink and takes a third impression.

7 In the finished print, the overprinting has produced a variety of tones and textures that create a simply stated but highly atmospheric image.

Linear drawing
1 Block-printing ink is rolled out thinly on the glass slab. The color areas are roughly estimated in relation to the subject to be drawn.

2 A sheet of paper is laid down over the ink, and the wooden end of a paintbrush is used to draw on the back of the paper. Alternatively you can use a pencil, knitting needle, or other suitable implement.

Developing textures
1 This experimental sequence investigates patterns and textures relating to water and wave patterns. Colored inks are squeezed onto the glass directly from the tube.

3 The impression shows a soft but strong line quality that gives an expressive character to the drawing. The background is lightly textured through contact with the rolled-out colors.

2 A simple blotting onto paper spreads the ink marks and produces a vigorously textured surface. There is always a random element to these very basic printing techniques.

3 The artist works into the painting on glass by blotting the colors again and adding fresh ink. The top band of the color layers is rolled out to create a feeling of the division between sea and sky.

4 Paper is placed over the ink, and using a pencil the artist begins to draw roughly scribbled wave patterns, working the hatched textures in different directions.

5 Progress can be checked at any stage by peeling back the paper; keep one edge in place so that the paper goes back in exactly the same position. If the image is not strong enough, the pressure of the pencil marks can be varied or reworked.

6 This impression has a looser, busier texture than the simple blotted-off image in step 2. The movements of the pencil create a more active surface in the finished print.

LINOCUT

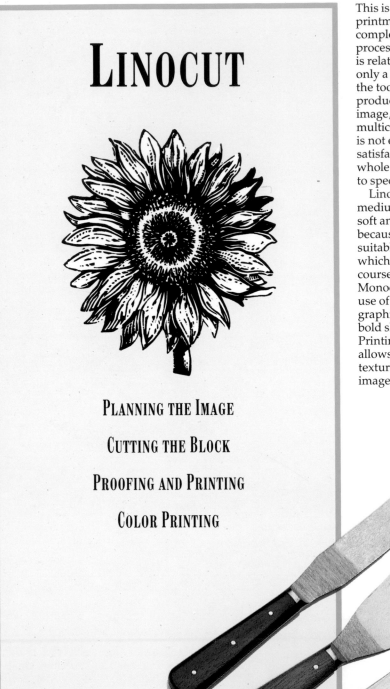

PLANNING THE IMAGE

CUTTING THE BLOCK

PROOFING AND PRINTING

COLOR PRINTING

This is an excellent printmaking technique for the complete beginner. The process of preparing the block is relatively simple, and after only a little experiment with the tools you can quickly produce a strikingly original image, either monochrome or multicolored. A printing press is not essential, so you can satisfactorily complete the whole process without access to specialized studio facilities.

Linoleum is a sympathetic medium in that it is relatively soft and easy to cut, but because of its pliability, it is not suitable for very fine line work, which can break down in the course of cutting or printing. Monochrome linocuts make use of the material's strong graphic potential, exploiting bold shapes and patterns. Printing in two or three colors allows many possibilities for texturing and shading the image.

Tools and materials

Linoleum is a corky, composite sheet material with a burlap backing. You can obtain small precut linoleum blocks from most art-supply stores, and large pieces or rolls up to 3 feet wide from specialist suppliers of printmaking materials.

The quality of linoleum varies; sometimes the block is very smooth and compact, but the texture can also be grainy and liable to crumble when cut. It deteriorates with age, becoming hard and brittle. Warming the block before you start cutting helps to soften a "difficult" texture, easing the passage of the tools. Linoleum has a naturally oily feel, but the surface can be degreased before you start work by wiping with denatured alcohol or rubbing gently with a fine-grade sandpaper.

The principal lino-cutting tools are gouges and V-tools of different sizes. You can also use an ordinary mat knife to cut grooves in the block or to outline areas to be cleared with the gouges. Blunt tools can easily tear the soft linoleum, so they should be kept sharp.

The block is inked with a roller. Different sizes and types are available, made of rubber, gelatine, or plastic. Inexpensive rollers are often too hard to give even coverage; a softer roller is more sensitive to any variations in the linoleum surface.

Linocut equipment

1, 2 Palette knife and ink spatula, for mixing inks; **3** knife for cutting linoleum; **4** spoon for hand-printing; **5** roller; **6** linoleum; **7** gouges; **8** V-tools; **9** baren, a custom-made tool for hand-printing.

5

6

9

7

8

Sharpening a gouge
1 Place the curved blade of the gouge on an oilstone and rock it from side to side so the whole edge makes contact with the stone.

2 Sharpen the inner edge of the blade with a broad slipstone. Support the tool firmly while rubbing the stone back and forth.

Sharpening a V-tool
1 Put one side of the blade flat on the oilstone and rub it back and forth. Repeat with the other side to sharpen both outer facets and the point between them.

2 To sharpen the inner edges, you need a fine slipstone that fits into the "V." Support the shaft of the tool as for the gouge, while moving the stone inside the blade.

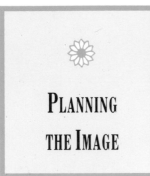

PLANNING THE IMAGE

You can mark out your design in pencil, marker, or India ink applied with brush or pen, de-greasing the surface first if necessary. If you are using a working drawing, you can trace this on the block using carbon transfer paper. Remember, however, that the image will appear reversed when printed; if you want it to read the same way around as the original, reverse the tracing before you transfer it to the block.

Alternatively, you can make the original drawing directly on the block, as shown here. If you make errors, you can either draw over them, remembering to ignore the incorrect lines when you begin to cut, or you can wipe out the error with a suitable solvent and rework the area completely.

Any shape in a linocut design can be cut positively or negatively: that is, you can cut around the outline of the shape or you can remove the whole area within the outline. When working in monochrome, you need to plan the interaction of lines and shapes carefully, working out what to do with the edges where two or more shapes butt together, and how to vary and contrast areas of solid color and pattern.

Gouge marks
The gouge makes a bold stroke that can be clean-edged or lightly toothed. This sample shows long and short cuts with (from left to right) medium-sized, fine, and broad gouges. The rough-edged mark is made by easing the tool from side to side, as well as forward through the linoleum.

V-tool marks
This sample shows a comparable group of marks made with medium-sized, fine, and broad V-tools. The beginning of the cut is slightly tapered where the "V" bites into the linoleum. You can end the cut with a taper by easing the tool up gradually, or you can form a squared end by stopping the stroke abruptly.

Developing texture
A more complex textured effect can be obtained by quite simple means when you are overprinting colors. This shows where the same marks of the V-tool have been recut more broadly for the black printing.

Line and tone
The tools can be used to cut the main shape in outline or to cut away the surrounding areas, leaving the outline in relief. You may even wish to combine the two approaches in one design and should plan how you will make the transition between solid shapes and line work.

Drawing on the block
1 For this demonstration of cutting a monochrome image, the artist works directly from the subject, drawing on the block with a black waxy pencil.

2 The markings on the fish form the most intricate part of the design, and they are drawn in some detail. The shape of the plate has been drawn to position the whole design on the center of the block.

3 The pattern on the plate is indicated very loosely, leaving the artist an open choice as to how to treat those areas as the cutting of the design develops.

CUTTING THE BLOCK

There is no particular order or sequence to cutting into the design. For example, you can begin with narrow cuts outlining the overall shapes, then work into detail and clear any large "white" areas; or you can work from one side to another, completing each section as you go. You will soon learn to judge which tools provide the right width of cut and how much pressure you need to apply. Avoid working too heavily, as it is easy to slip and cut into a section that should be left uncut. Move the tool easily and evenly; if you angle a knife or V-tool blade too sharply, you may undercut the linoleum, which makes lines and edges unstable.

If you have a large area to clear which is "non-reading" in the print, or you are shaping the outer edges of the block, you need not do all the work with the gouges. You can cut away the surplus linoleum with a mat knife or scissors.

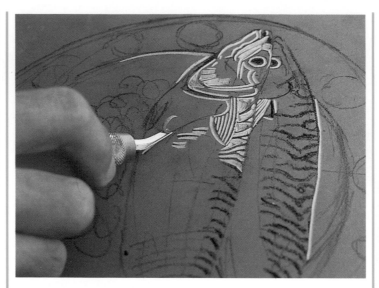

Cutting the block
1 Initially a V-tool is used to establish fine outlines and work into the detail of the fish head and body.

2 Once the markings of both fish have been described with careful line work, the artist begins to clear the "white" areas, working rapidly with a broad gouge.

3 The gouge is used roughly so that the lowered surface of the block retains some relief texture that will print.

4 The outer border around the design is not to print at all. Rather than clear it with a gouge, the artist cuts the linoleum away. The shape of the plate is outlined with a V-tool, then cuts are made from the edge toward the outline.

5 The edge-cuts make the linoleum more flexible, allowing the scissors to ease accurately around the circular shape. If the border area were cut with a gouge, some residual marks might appear on the print, but removing the surplus guarantees a clean outline.

PROOFING AND PRINTING

For a monochrome print like the example shown here, you can check the progress of the cutting without actually rolling up and printing the block. Simply place a piece of paper over the surface and take a rubbing with a pencil. This will be accurate enough to show you where further cutting is required, and whether there is a good balance of negative and positive areas.

When the block is ready to print, roll out the ink thinly on the inking slab, then roll it over the raised areas of the linoleum firmly and evenly. You can work back and forth in all directions, and if you put down too much ink, you can take up some of the excess by running the roller in one direction only.

You can take a print either by placing paper over the block and rubbing with a baren, a spoon, or any other suitable smooth, curved tool; or you can print on a flat-bed, cylinder, or proofing press.

Proofing and printing
1 Rather than ink the block to pull a proof, the artist takes a rubbing on thin paper with a graphite pencil. Any refinements needed can be cleanly cut before printing.

4 Position the inked block on a clean sheet of paper on the bed of the press. Align the printing paper to the base sheet, so the printed image will be centrally placed, and lower the paper onto the block.

2 When the design is complete, it can be inked and printed. To roll ink out evenly, spread it across the glass slab with a palette knife, then work outward with the roller until the ink forms a thin coating.

3 You can work in all directions when rolling up the block. Go over it as many times as you need to coat it evenly with color, picking up more ink on the roller as necessary.

5 Activate the press to exert even pressure on the block and paper. Take hold of one corner of the printing paper and peel it back gently from the block.

Printing without a press

1 If you have no access to a press, you can use this hand-printing method, also known as burnishing. Ink the block and position it on a clean base sheet. Lay the printing paper over it.

2 Use a rounded implement such as a custom-built baren, the back of a spoon, or as here, an etching dauber wrapped in cheesecloth, to rub firmly and evenly all over the back of the printing sheet.

3 A print taken by this method is naturally lighter colored than one taken on a press, because the pressure is less intense. As you continue to take prints and the ink layer on the block builds up, the image becomes darker and more even.

6 The completed print has a bold, graphic style, with crisp black line work nicely offset by the incidental patches of rough texture in the whites. Variations in the line widths give a pleasing "hand-done" quality without detracting from the clarity of the image.

COLOR PRINTING

Multicolored linocuts can be prepared by one of two methods. In the reduction process, successive cuts are made in the same block, and a new color is printed at various stages. The other method is to register the design on separate blocks, one for each color. The reduction method* (demonstrated under woodcut printing), may be easier to register for printing, as it is the same block you are using at each stage; but the block is gradually destroyed by the continuing work, so you have to be confident about how much of the surface is to be removed for each printing.

Using two or more blocks gives you more time to think through the cutting stages, and you can proof all the colors to compare and amend the different areas. However, any slight variations in the dimensions or shape of the blocks' outer edges can make it difficult to align each printing.

To cut two or more blocks, you can use a master tracing to place the image on each, but a more accurate method is to cut the first block and use it as the key block for offsetting the image onto the uncut linoleum pieces. As shown here, the method used to register block and paper for the offsetting is then also used to register the overprintings.

FURTHER INFORMATION

*Woodcuts: Color printing, page 40–45

Offsetting and overprinting
1 Cut your block for the first color, using the appropriate marks and textures for the effect you wish to achieve.

2 Ink up the first block in black and lay it centered on a clean sheet of paper on the bed of the press. With a pencil, mark the edges and corners of the block on the base sheet. This sheet will form your guide for registering subsequent printings. Pull a print from the block on smooth paper.

Registering on the press
This method of registration is a simple alternative to the use of a base sheet, as shown in the main sequence. Mark the positions for the block and printing paper directly on the bed of the press, using small strips of cardboard attached with masking tape. Butt the corner of the block to the inner cards. Next slip the corner of the paper in to align with the outer registration stops before lowering the full sheet over the block.

3 Lay the uncut second block in the marked area on the base sheet and place the black print over it, aligned to the edges of the base sheet. Run this through the press so that the print transfers color onto the clean linoleum block.

7 Roll up the second block in the required color – in this example it is to print black over red. Position the block on the base sheet, register the printed image over it, and run them through the press.

4 Use the shapes offset from the first block as a guide to cutting your design for the second color. Pay special attention to areas where the two colors will overprint, and any shapes that must register exactly.

5 Roll up and print the first block in the required color. Here it is printed in red: this is the same block that was printed black in steps 2 and 3 to offset the image.

6 You may find it helpful to mark one corner of the base sheet and the corresponding corner of the print with a small cross: each time you come to print, from a second or subsequent block, match the crosses and then align from that corner. This is particularly valuable when you are printing several colors, as the prints can appear quite abstract in the early stages, and it is easy to make an error in overprinting.

8 This extremely lively image combines solid blocks of color with roughly worked gouged textures and bold patterns made with the V-tool. The registration of colors on the figure is deliberately inexact to add to the sense of movement, but where required, background shapes have overprinted cleanly along the same outlines.

WOODCUT

CUTTING THE BLOCK

COLOR PRINTING

Woodcut printing is very similar in technique and process to linocut, but different in style and surface quality due to the properties of the base material. Woodcuts are made on the side grain of the wood, and the natural pattern and direction of the grain are integrated with the textures and patterns made by the cutting process.

In linocutting, the tools cut easily in all directions, but for woodcuts it is easier to cut along or with the grain than across or against it. The type of wood used – how heavily grained and hard or soft it is – will also affect the print. You can obtain interesting variations between clean and ragged edges, sharp knife cuts, or broadly gouged channels. Woodcuts are associated with the aggressive, jagged graphics of European Expressionists, but also with the clarity and formality of Japanese color prints, so a wide range of variations is possible.

Tools and materials
A useful aspect of the woodcut process for beginners is that you can use almost any type of wood. Instead of buying specially prepared blocks you can pick up offcuts of plywood or timber from a lumberyard. Pine boards and plywood sheets, inexpensive and readily available, are highly suitable for trying out the cutting techniques and gaining confidence with the medium. They are relatively coarse and liable to splinter, but are also soft to cut and have pleasing, pronounced grain patterns. As you become interested in the process of woodcut and practiced in the techniques, you can investigate finer,

denser woods that allow more delicate control. The only way to discover and exploit the characteristics of different wood types is to try them.

Tools for woodcut include the V-tools and gouges used for linocut. The interchangeable gouge sets, however, are unsuitable as they are not strong enough; use individual metal-shafted gouges. Cutting knives are extensively used in woodcut; specialist tools are available from printmaking suppliers or you can use a sturdy mat knife. Chisels are also useful tools for abrading the surface and clearing large areas.

Prints are made from wood blocks in exactly the same way as from linoleum; the surface is inked and the print can be taken by hand or on a press. Thin plywood can be printed on a cylinder or flat-bed press. A thick wood block must be printed by the direct pressure of a flat-bed press, or on a type-proofing press where the block can be packed into a sunken bed and the paper rolled over it.

Woodcut equipment
1 Side-grain wood blocks; **2** gouges and V-tools; **3** mat knife; **4** cutting knife, for fine-line work on block; **5, 6** ink spatula and palette knife; **7** block-printing ink.

5

6

4

3

7

2

1

CUTTING THE BLOCK

Some artists cut directly into the block without preparation. Others may prepare the surface by sandpapering or brushing with a wire brush to remove any loose fibers and bring up the grain pattern. As with linoleum, you can draw onto the surface with pencils, markers, or brush and ink, or trace a design using transfer paper. You can, if you wish, stain the surface all over by rubbing it with diluted printing ink; this enables you to see the cut marks as you progress.

Wood is quite a responsive surface, and you can obtain good effects from a variety of different marks. Try to get the feel of the tool as you cut, particularly as you change its angle to the grain. Pushing a gouge easily along the grain produces even, clean-edged cuts, but cutting too boldly across it can cause major splintering that strips too much of the surface.

The width of the gouge you choose has to be matched to the elements of your design, but otherwise the choice of tool is a matter of common sense – there is obviously more work involved in trying to clear a large area with a narrow gouge than with a wide one. In an open area, you may leave small ridges that will print as a broken texture; this can be effective, but if after proofing you find it is not suitable, you can clean up the shape and remove any cutting marks.

Cutting the block
1 Unless your design is small-scale, or you are very confident in cutting, it is best to draw a fairly detailed outline of the image on the wood block.

Using gouges
1 All woodcut tools cut most easily along the grain of the wood. A small gouge makes clean-edged fine lines suitable for outlining or hatched textures.

2 The print shows how the grain of the wood contributes a specific background texture, where the relief surface is allowed to print as large areas of dark tone.

3 Broad gouges are used for line work. In addition, by keeping the cuts very close together or overlapping them, broad gouges can be used to clear areas of the block.

4 Pushing the gouge across rather than along the grain, you encounter more resistance and may need to ease the gouge from side to side as it moves forward.

2 In this example the image depends upon some intricate pattern-making in the structures of the buildings. The artist draws this in detail, filling in lines and shapes that feature strongly.

4 Because the print will consist of a four color sequence, the cutting at this stage is relatively limited, consisting only of those elements that will appear white in the final print. Fine detail is worked with a narrow gouge.

3 She begins cutting the broadest lines, stripping the wood rapidly with a gouge. As with linoleum, there is no particular rule as to where you should start.

5 Although the width of the tool mark does not vary much, you can see how working along or across the grain produces different edge qualities.

6 The V-tool reacts similarly to the gouge in terms of the direction it takes. However, if the angled blade is sharp, the cross-grain resistance may be less influential because the cutting edge is less broad.

7 A V-tool cut begins sharply and broadens as the full width of the blade bites into the wood. Short, angular cuts produce interesting coarse textures.

8 The actual character of each mark may be less important than the way the tools are used to cut particular elements in the design, but this sample block demonstrates a wide range of textures obtained with only three tools.

COLOR PRINTING

This demonstration shows a four-color wood block cut and printed by the reduction method. In the first cutting, only the areas to remain white are taken out, and the block is printed with the first color rolled all over the surface. In the second stage, the areas to remain as the first color – in this case a light buff – are removed, and the whole block is printed in yellow. In the third stage, areas to remain yellow are cut out and the block is printed in blue. Finally, the blue areas are cut away, and the remaining relief surface is overprinted in black.

With the reduction method, it is not necessary to follow the process of offsetting demonstrated for linocut, but you can use the same registration process to make sure that the colors overprint accurately. In this case, however, having printed the first color, the artist registers the block for each subsequent printing by laying it face down on the print rather than aligning the paper over the block. For this you need a confident eye and steady hands.

Printing and overprinting
1 When the first stage of cutting is complete, you can immediately print the first color (you may wish to take one proof first to check the balance of the image and the effectiveness of individual shapes). Roll up the whole block with an even layer of ink.

2 Run the print through the press and peel back the paper carefully. Once you have begun to lift the paper, it is advisable not to lay it back down, as any slight shift can create a double image.

3 At the second cutting stage, remove all areas of the block that will appear as the first color – in this case, beige – in the final print.

4 If you have to mix a special color when printing, make sure you have a quantity that will cover the number of prints you wish to make; it can be difficult to match a mixed hue.

5 Roll up the block in the second color, working in all directions to produce an even coating of ink. It is advisable to have a roller that relates well to the size of the block. A large brayer is being used here.

6 To register the second color over the first, the artist lays the block face down on the original print, judging the alignment of edges and corners by eye.

7 The cutting in the third stage consists of removing all the areas of the image that should appear yellow in the final print. An experienced artist may work directly on the block; for a beginner, it is helpful to use a previously prepared color study as a guide.

8 There may be a lot of detailed cutting at the final stage, because in order to allow the previous three colors to show through, much of the remaining relief surface becomes linear in character.

9 Large areas of the block have now been cleared, particularly the sky, which is very open. The cutting is deliberately rough, so that a lightly textured impression will show up between the more emphatic lines.

Stage proof: two
The second color printing begins to suggest the three-dimensional depth in the image, but because the two colors are close in tone, the change is not dramatic.

Stage proof: one
In a print made by the reduction method, the first color printing may include a lot of broad, flat color areas where the detail will be created by the cutting for subsequent colors. When printing is completed, clean the ink from the block immediately with solvent and a rag.

Stage proof: four

The black printing sharpens the image and gives it a much bolder, more graphic feeling, pulling together all the shapes. This is the effect that the artist has been carrying in her mind throughout the cutting processes. The radical changes that occur with each successive stage are a very exciting feature of color printing. Although with experience you can anticipate many aspects of the color interactions, the overall result can still contain surprising and unexpectedly pleasing details.

Stage proof: three

The overprinting in blue, using the same registration technique as for the yellow, produces a more appreciable variation in the image, both because the color is lighter than those underneath and because the textures are becoming more complex.

WOOD ENGRAVING

CUTTING THE BLOCK

PROOFING AND PRINTING

Wood engraving is a much finer, more delicate process than woodcut. The cutting is done on the end-grain of the wood, which has a very tight texture. The grain is not a feature of the design – the image is created entirely by the cut marks.

The techniques of wood engraving are controlled and precise, but you can achieve a wide variety of marks and textures. For practical reasons wood engravings are usually small scale, and it is easier to produce an image that reads as white lines on black than to clear areas of the block leaving black lines in relief. It is typically a monochrome method (although the relief surface can be inked in any color) since the engraved work is too detailed and tight to allow the processes of re-cutting and overprinting that can be exploited with side-grain wood and linoleum. Printing in black, or a very dark-toned color, best conveys the subtle graphic effects of the engraving.

Tools and materials

The preferred wood for end-grain blocks is box, which has a tight grain, but is relatively soft and easy to engrave. This is a slow-growing, small tree, so wood-engraving blocks are usually only 2–3 inches across – larger blocks are made by jointing small pieces together. They are expensive, and you need to obtain the blocks from a specialist supplier, as the wood must be properly seasoned and prepared. Holly, pear, or maple, cheaper substitutes, may also be available. In addition, compact blocks of plywood or manufactured board can be used.

The engraving tools are fine shafts of metal faceted and sharpened to form various shapes of cutting tip. The main types are the lozenge-shaped graver for general line work, the elliptical graver, designed for cutting curves; the squared or rounded scorper, used for broad marks and clearing areas of the block; and the fine tint tool, which maintains a line of

1

uniform width. It is important to keep the tools sharp, as blunt tools slip and slide on the close-grained surface.

To cut curves and angles you turn the block rather than the tool. To facilitate the movement, it can be mounted on a traditional engraver's sandbag, but you can work just as effectively by resting the block on a book wrapped in a cloth. Raising the block also helps you to grip it and hold it steady.

The block-printing ink for wood engraving should be quite stiff, or it may flood the delicate marks. A small gelatine or rubber roller is adequate for inking the little wood blocks. Prints can be taken easily by hand-burnishing using a spoon or baren to rub the back of the paper.

3

4

5

2

6

Wood engraving equipment
1 End-grain wood blocks; **2** engraving tools; **3** glass mixing slab; **4** block-printing ink; **5** palette knife; **6** roller.

Holding the tools

1 Fit the mushroom-shaped wooden handle of the tool into your palm and support the metal shaft lightly with your fingers. Grip the shaft close to the cutting tip with index finger and thumb.

2 For engraving straight lines and curves, keep the tool at a shallow angle to the working surface, allowing the pressure of your whole hand to move it forward.

3 For short cuts, such as fine and coarse stippling, raise the tool at a sharper angle so that the action of the cutting tip is naturally abbreviated.

Marks of the tools
This test block and print show some of the variations of texture that can be achieved with different tools handled in different ways. On the print, these are: (top, left to right) stippling with a coarse graver; dashes cut with an elliptical graver; close stippling with a fine graver; (bottom, left to right) short cuts with a scorper; lines cut with a scorper; lines cut with an elliptical graver.

Sharpening tools
1 To sharpen a graver, put the face of the cutting tip flat down on the oilstone and rub with a circular motion.

2 To sharpen a scorper, put the underside of the cutting tip on the oilstone and move it back and forth. Repeat with both flat sides of the narrow blade.

CUTTING THE BLOCK

A drawing can be made directly on the block, or a prepared design can be traced down. If you are working in a way that produces a white-line image, you may find it easiest to darken the surface of the block with ink. You can then make your tracing with white transfer paper, so that the initial drawing corresponds to what you expect to see in the print.

For line work, the tool is held at a shallow angle to the block; the shape is designed for this, with the shaft broadly angled away from the wooden handle. The cutting needs to be quite slow and precise: because you are working on a small area, a too-forceful stroke can cause a significant error.

Drawing on the block
1 Paint the upper surface of the block with a thin coat of black drawing ink and allow it to dry completely.

2 Place a piece of white or light colored transfer paper on the block and put your drawing over it. Tape it to the edge of the block and go over the design in pencil to trace it.

3 The transferred drawing in white on black gives an idea of the way the print will appear, but you do not need to fill in all the detail at this stage – this can be developed as you cut.

Cutting the block
1 Support the block on a raised surface while you cut, so you can hold it firmly by its edges. A book wrapped in cloth is the support used here.

3 The scorper is used to draw strong lines and to clear small areas of the block; note the shallow angle of the tip on the surface.

2 Work into different areas of the design with the appropriate tool. This picture shows a graver being used for stippled detail.

4 Work the cutting to a more or less finished stage before taking a proof. Most of the detail should be in place, with only minor refinements to do after proofing.

PROOFING AND PRINTING

Once you have inked the block to take a proof, it is less easy to see the design clearly, as the ink will have stained some of the finer lines. Proofing is thus best left until the work is quite advanced. You can then make any refinements needed in the cutting before you take final prints. Do not clean off the ink with a solvent after proofing – just wipe it with a rag to remove the excess.

In keeping with the overall character of the process, the method of inking should be careful and controlled. You need only make one pass of the roller over the block in each direction. It is important not to over-ink the relief surface or the color will spread into and fill the engraved lines.

Proofing and printing
1 Roll out the ink on a glass mixing slab. Use quite a stiff block-printing ink so it will not flood the delicate lines cut into the wood block.

2 Roll up the surface of the block, being careful not to over-ink. You need only make one pass of the roller in each direction across the surface.

3 Use a lightweight printing paper that will pick up all the detail. Because the block is small, it is easy to pull the proof by burnishing with the back of a small spoon. Place the paper on the block and rub it firmly.

4 When you see the result of the proof, you can decide what further work is necessary before final prints are taken. Here, the artist decides some extra highlighting is needed.

5 Before continuing to cut, wipe the excess ink off the block with a clean rag. Do not use a solvent, as this will flood the cuts and stain them, making it difficult to see the design.

6 As the final stage on this engraving, the artist uses a graver to cut a halo of fine stippling around the butterfly shape (below).

7 This attractive image demonstrates the small-scale character of wood engraving and the way it is necessary to balance the tones and textures by controlling the weight and direction of the various marks.

COLLAGE BLOCKS

9

This area of printmaking provides the opportunity to produce interesting and varied printed images without use of specialist materials and tools. The basic principle of relief printing, in which the design is formed by the contrast between positive (raised) areas of the printing block and negative (cut-away) sections, can be adapted to handmade blocks constructed from a wide range of materials. These are assembled on a flat base to form a relief block with different surface levels. Suitable materials include paper, cardboard, fabric, and string; objects such as bottle tops and buttons; or acrylic

mediums, which are applied in fluid form and dry to form hard, rubbery textures.

The technique has the same relationship to linocut or woodcut as collage has to painting. Instead of manipulating one material to create your effects, you combine different substances and textures. You ink with a roller as if it were a wood or linoleum block. To print, you can use the hand-burnishing* method of rubbing the paper down onto the inked block with a spoon or similar tool, though a relief printing press gives you a stronger, denser image.

The term collograph refers to a collaged block printed in the

2

1

same way as an intaglio plate*. To print the block effectively, it must be run through an intaglio printing press, so the collage should not be too thick – about ¼ inch – so it will easily pass between the rollers.

Tools and materials

The only tools you need are a mat knife and scissors for cutting your materials and a roller for inking up the block. Choosing materials for the collage is a matter of judgment and experience. It is not possible to predict absolutely the effect a particular material will make. Sometimes the roller picks up much more or less of the surface texture than you anticipate, though you can adjust the effects a little in the pressures you apply to inking up and printing. It is useful to experiment with small samples before selecting materials for a particular kind of image.

Among the simplest and most readily available materials are different kinds of chip and mat boards, and papers – you can save offcuts and packaging materials, looking for varied weights and textures. String, yarn, ribbon, and braid are all effective. Adhesive tape is useful for forming linear and geometric motifs.

An all-purpose adhesive such as PVA (craft glue) works as both the means of gluing materials to the support and as an independent printing element. The viscous white medium can be thickly applied with a pen, brush, or knife; it dries into a clear, rubbery surface that retains its original texture and prints well. It also makes an excellent binder for loose-textured materials such as sand or rice.

The number of impressions you can take depends upon the resilience of the materials you have used – the surface will eventually break down, especially if some of the materials are absorbent. Sealing the surface with a thin application of polymer acrylic medium makes the collage more durable.

Equipment for collage blocks
1 Buttons; **2** wood shavings; **3** dried beans, peas, or rice; **4** yarn; **5** pasta; **6** PVA adhesive; **7** scissors; **8** mat knives; **9** paper and cardboard.

FURTHER INFORMATION

*Linocuts: Proofing and printing, pages 31–33
*Intaglio printing: inking and wiping; pulling the print, pages 106–107

Braid and yarn
Scraps of fancy braid and yarns from a knitting or sewing basket contribute unusual pattern qualities. Because the materials are absorbent, you may need to ink and print a few times before the full impression comes through.

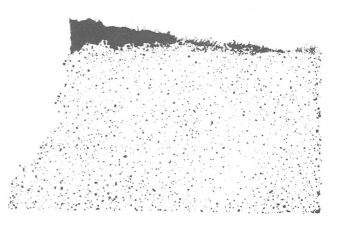

Cardboard
In addition to selecting different textures and thicknesses of cardboard to create variations in your print, you can cut into the surface and peel back the top layer to make hard edges and rough, broken textures.

Sandpaper
The gritty surface of sandpaper prints a fine pattern of irregular dots. The solid color at the top edge of this section comes from tearing the material so that the abrasive layer is pulled away, leaving only the base paper.

String

Pieces of string create distinct, fine lines, but with a pleasing burred texture. Different effects will be obtained according to the weight and thickness of the string and the fibers from which it is made.

Tape

Masking tape has a rough finish that prints as a mottled or striated texture. Smooth, finer tapes allow the ink to print more evenly. The edges print as dark or light lines, depending on the thickness of the tape.

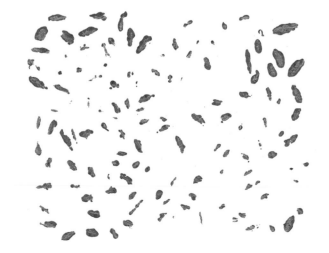

Split peas

Loose materials such as dried peas, beans or rice, sand, or wood chips can be glued to the collage base by pressing them into a layer of acrylic medium and allowing it to dry. The patterns that print are more random than you might expect, in this case because the dried peas have irregular surfaces.

Rice

A hand-proofed print from a layer of rice stuck in acrylic medium produces a coarse stipple effect. With all such materials, you will obtain a slightly stronger texture if you print on a press, because of the more intense, even contact between printing surface and paper.

Glue painting

1 A thick acrylic glue can be painted on cardboard in rough shapes and drawn into with the wooden end of the paintbrush, or with a pencil. The medium is opaque white while wet, so you can see what you are doing, but dries clear.

Making the collage

1 The materials are glued to a cardboard base; let the glue dry completely before printing. This example is a hilly landscape constructed from various thicknesses and finishes of cardboard, sandpaper, string, and crumpled tissue paper for the sky.

2 Because the medium is applied in liquid form, the surface areas are slightly curved, which becomes more apparent as the glue painting dries. In this case only the highest ridges have printed, giving the effect of a free, bold line drawing.

2 In the first proof, the softer cardboard layers reveal a "honeycomb" texture under the pressure of printing. This appears too evenly distributed and mechanical, so additional materials are added to the block.

3 This proof has a more satisfactory contrast of textured and solid color areas. In the foreground, thin cardboard pieces create strong black shapes; the upper slopes of the hills are more densely textured where a thick layer of acrylic medium has been loosely brushed on.

SCREENPRINTING

HAND-CUT STENCILS

PAPER STENCILS

FILLER STENCILS

TUSCHE METHOD

The principle of screenprinting is somewhat different from that of the other printmaking processes in that the print is taken not by the direct impression of one surface upon another, but by printing through an intermediary surface – the screen mesh. The images of screenprints are formed by various kinds of stenciling techniques, based on blocking out areas of the mesh either with sheet materials such as paper or stencil film or with liquids that fill the mesh.

In addition to being a fine-art process, screenprinting has a direct association with commercial and industrial printing processes, being used extensively in graphic, ceramic, and textile design. It is a colorful, versatile medium which you can adapt to the context of your work.

Tools and materials

The basic equipment consists of the screen – a wooden frame with a fine-mesh fabric stretched over it – and the squeegee. This is a rubber blade set in a handle, with which the screen ink is pulled across the mesh. The mesh transmits an even coating of ink which adheres to the paper below the screen.

The stencil, whatever its form, seals certain areas of the screen so that the ink cannot pass through, thus creating positive and negative color areas. The stencil can be a material as simple as thin paper that will adhere to the underside of the mesh – for example, newsprint or tracing paper. Stencil film is a gelatinous material on a plastic backing that can be cut with a sharp mat knife – when soaked with water it softens and is pressed into the mesh before the backing is removed. A similar effect can be obtained with self-adhesive plastic film applied to the screen, and you can also use adhesive tape. Paper and film stencils produce clean-cut, hard-edged images.

2

6

Materials that are precut and then applied to the screen are known as indirect stencils, while those which are applied by painting and drawing are called direct stencils. "Liquid stencils," or screen fillers, may be water-soluble, oil-based, or cellulose. The type you use depends on the type of ink, as the filler must remain resistant to the solvent of the ink so that the stencil remains intact when you print and clean the ink from the screen. Commonly, water-based fillers are used in combination with oil-based inks*. Conversely, you can combine oil-based filler with water-based inks. Cellulose filler is impervious to both oil- and water-based inks, but has to be cleaned from the mesh with a special solvent.

FURTHER INFORMATION

*Screenprinting: filler stencils, page 70–73

Screenprinting equipment
1 Squeegee; 2 screen; 3 screenprinting inks; 4 palette knife; 5 solvent brush to remove stencils; 6 cleaning rags.

1

3

5

4

HAND-CUT
STENCILS

The advantage of using hand-cut stencils is that all the elements of the printed image are prepared away from the screen. If you get something completely wrong, you can remake the stencil. When cutting film stencils, you can see through the material, so it can be placed over a working drawing to guide the cutting.

When you plan the image, you must take into account that paper or film stencils give you hard-edged, graphic shapes. Each color to be printed requires a separate stencil. If the ink is fairly transparent, you can obtain color "mixtures" by overprinting one hue on another, and build up quite complex effects of pattern and form by varying the shapes and details of each overprinting. The process of registering color printings on the screen bed is quite simple.

Where color areas are to be butted together, you should allow a very tiny overlap when cutting the separate stencils for each color, as otherwise you may get a white line between them as you print the colors individually. The demonstration sequence shows both the processes of preparing hand-cut stencils and the basic methods of inking and printing. The simple technique of laying out ink and pulling the squeegee across the mesh is standard no matter how the screen stencils are prepared.

Preparing hand-cut stencils
1 Stencil film has two layers – the colored stencil and a clear backing sheet. Use a fine scalpel or mat knife to cut lightly into the top layer. Here the artist is using a working sketch slipped under the stencil as a guide.

2 When you have cut a shape in outline, use the point of the knife to lift one edge or corner, then peel back the cut shape.

3 Prepare stencils for each of the colors you are to print and check that the shapes align by overlaying them on top of another. In this demonstration, six colors are to be printed: pink, yellow, light blue, red, medium blue, black.

4 Position the stencil under the screen mesh. Because a large screen is used here, and the stencils are relatively small, the artist is placing three stencils side by side on one screen.

5 Lower the screen so the mesh lies flat on the stencil and spray clean water on the mesh. This softens the stencil material so it will adhere to the screen. You must move quickly to the next stage.

6 Lay a clean piece of newsprint over the screen and blot firmly with your hands, creating pressure that sticks the stencil to the mesh. Because this has to be done quickly, if you are putting more than one stencil on the screen, do each in turn rather than all together.

7 When all of the stencils adhere to the screen, allow them to dry completely. You can speed up the process by using a hot-air dryer.

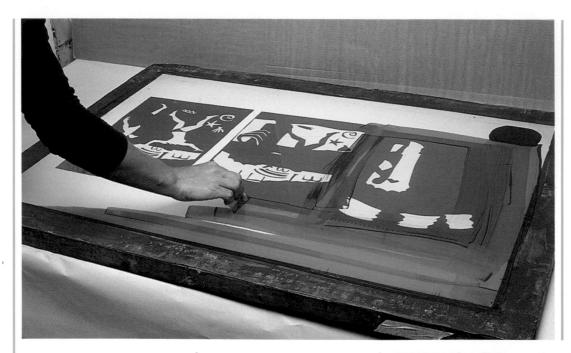

8 To block out the open areas of the screen mesh surrounding the stencils, turn the screen upside down and spread a liquid filler around the borders.

The simplest way to do this is to use a small piece of mat board to pull the liquid across the mesh.

9 Any errors on the stencil can be blocked out in the same way. Here the artist fills in a shape that is not intended to appear in the color that this stencil will be printing.

Printing technique
1 This demonstration shows printing on a screen frame attached to a vacuum-bed printing table. The screen is securely locked into the frame.

4 If you have more than one stencil on the screen, use paper to cover those not printing at this stage. This keeps them clean and prevents ink from bleeding through beyond the first stencil.

7 When the paper is in the correct position, the left-hand lower corner and edge are marked with pieces of masking tape stuck to the screen bed. The printing paper will be positioned against these guides each time the first color is printed.

8 Mix your ink colors in sufficient quantity to allow for the required number of prints. Screenprinting ink is a thick liquid and is commonly mixed in paper cups; any leftovers can be stored this way.

2 The plastic backing on the stencils must be removed before they can be used to print. Take hold of one edge and peel the backing off smoothly.

5 You need to put registration marks on the screen bed so the image is correctly positioned on the paper. The artist uses the original working sketch to locate the printing area.

6 The sketch is moved around until it is accurately aligned with the stencil image. This picture shows the screen lowered and the artist checking the alignment through the mesh.

3 Tape the edges of the screen all around to form a reservoir for the ink and make sure that no color bleeds under the mesh where it joins the screen frame. You can use gummed paper or self-adhesive tape.

9 Pour the ink in an even flow across the bottom border of the screen, below the image. It puddles outward but, because it is viscous, does not flow into the stencil area.

10 Lift the screen slightly and use the squeegee to push the ink back across the mesh, flooding the color into the image area.

11 Position the clean piece of printing paper on the screen bed, aligned to the register marks previously taped in place. Lower the screen over the paper.

12 Place the squeegee in the layer of ink at the top of the screen and pull it firmly and evenly across the image area. You must use a squeegee that covers the entire width of the stencil, and keep it firmly horizontal as you pull.

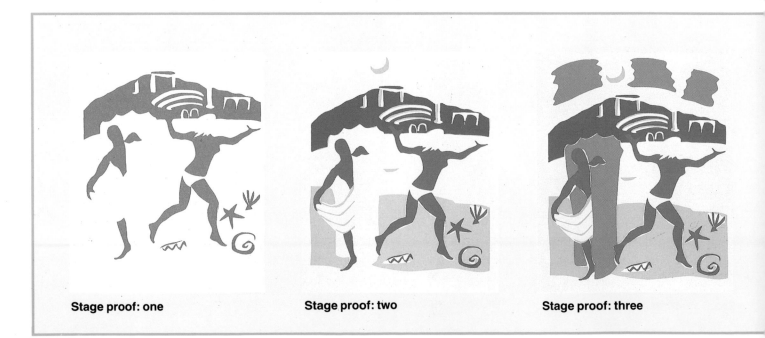

Stage proof: one

Stage proof: two

Stage proof: three

Registering overprintings
1 To register the second and subsequent colors quickly and accurately, the artist uses an acetate sheet attached to the screen bed on one side. The single color is printed on the acetate. Then the print is placed underneath.

2 The print is moved around until it aligns exactly with the newly printed color on the acetate. Then the positions of the bottom corner and left-hand edge are marked with tapes on the screen bed, as before.

Stage proofs
This sequence (below) shows how the image develops new form and depth with each color printing. Notice, in the second stage, that the overprinting of transparent yellow on pink has produced a "mixed" color – a warm orange. Although each stencil image consists of hard-edged shapes, the artist has successfully achieved a free, lively style of image by using small shapes and patterns to break up the broad color areas. She keeps the final, black printing very linear, to sharpen the detail.

Stage proof: four

Stage proof: five

Stage proof: six

PAPER STENCILS

Using newsprint or tracing paper for your stencils is ideal for the beginner in one respect – it enables you to experiment inexpensively. However, remember that a paper stencil is naturally less durable than film. You can draw direct on paper or trace from an original drawing and cut with knife or scissors. The paper pieces laid on the screen bed adhere to the mesh with the first pass of squeegee and ink, so you do not need to have links between all the shapes. "Floating" pieces must be positioned carefully at the start, but will then become self-adhesive.

Even if you keep to a fairly simple design, you can create exciting variations by trying different ways of inking. Color blends and variegations are easy to form on a screen. This demonstration also shows the use of talcum powder to obtain a mottled texture: the powder is pressed into the mesh at the first inking and forms a block in the same way as a sheet material or liquid filler.

Paper stencil
1 A simple design, a starburst with an animal figure inside, is freely cut from newsprint. You can use freestanding shapes within a paper screen stencil, as each piece adheres to the screen mesh individually.

3 Lay out the ink along the bottom of the screen. To make a blend of colors, pour a small pool of each color and let them flow gently together.

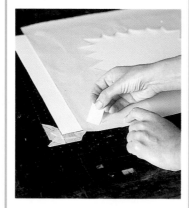

2 Position the printing paper on the screen bed and mark the corner. Lay the paper stencil over it in the required position. You can put pieces of double-sided tape at the corners to help attach the stencil to the screen.

4 Lift the screen and flood the color back into the mesh by pushing the squeegee upward. Then lower the screen and pull the other way to make the print.

8 It is easy and economical to experiment using these techniques. This example has been printed using the discarded section cut out of the previous stencil. The giraffe appears this time as a positive image, while the starburst is the negative shape.

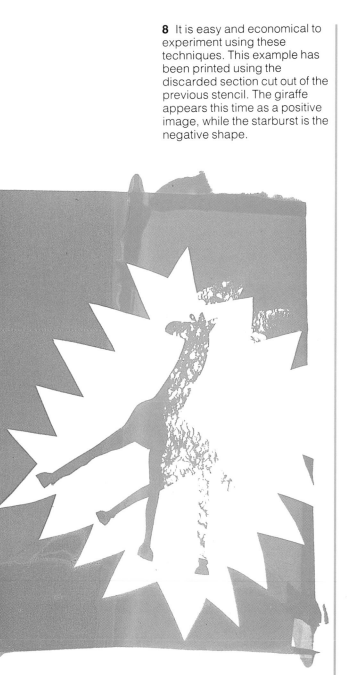

5 The starburst shape and the cutout of the giraffe can be seen sticking to the underside of the mesh, while their silhouettes are clearly printed on the paper in the warm color blend.

6 To add texture using talcum powder, make a paper stencil outlining the shape to be printed and attach it to the screen. Shake talc freely but loosely onto the print.

7 Lower the screen and print the required color in the usual way. The movement of the squeegee presses the talc into the screen mesh, acting as a block to the ink. This forms a random, lacy pattern.

FILLER STENCILS

Painting on the screen mesh with liquid filler is a satisfyingly direct way of working, enabling you to produce freer and more painterly effects. The main drawback for the inexperienced printmaker is that the design has to be worked out negatively – the brushmarks create the non-printing areas. However, because you can see through the screen mesh, you can place a working drawing underneath to guide you as you paint the stencil image; then it is only a matter of concentration.

This demonstration sequence also shows how effectively you can utilize overprintings of semi-transparent colors. The artist uses the process printing colors – cyan (blue), magenta (red), and yellow – with a final overprinting in white. She achieves dark shades such as green and purple, as well as tints of pale blue and pink. This is the same principle as applied in commercial printing, where variable combinations of the process colors achieve an almost infinite color range – the color photographs in this book are printed using only cyan, magenta, yellow, and black.

Using filler
1 When painting the filler directly onto the screen mesh, you may find it easiest to place a working drawing or sketch under the mesh as a guide, as shown here.

2 In this example, the artist begins with a stencil that will print blue. To allow for overprintings that will form mixed hues, only the flowers and outline pattern on the vase are blocked out.

3 The second color to be printed is red. Only those areas to remain pure blue are blocked out. The artist applies a sponged texture to the foreground area.

4 The background will remain blue and is fully blocked out, leaving the shapes of the flowers, vase, and tabletop to print in red.

Stage proof: one
The first printing (left) shows broad areas of fairly solid, uniform color with little detail visible at this stage.

Stage proof: two
Where the red has overprinted on the original blue (right), a rich, deep blue-purple is formed that gives depth and weight to the image. Flashes of the white paper remain where the mesh has been blocked out on both stencils.

(Stage proofs continued on page 73.)

5 The same process is applied to preparing and printing the third stage of the image – the transparent yellow layer.

6 White ink will be used in the last stage, to vary the shades and enhance the textures. The artist prepares the final stencil exactly, by working to the existing print placed underneath the screen.

7 The white ink is flooded onto the screen and the print is pulled by drawing the squeegee downward.

(Stage proofs continued from page 71.)

Stage proof: three
The yellow overprints on both the blue and red, producing green and scarlet respectively (left). This completely transforms not only the color balance of the image, but also the description of the shapes.

Stage proof: four
The white ink creates paler shades of all the original colors, and where it is printed over red and blue, it makes a neutral, warm gray (right). Using only four colors, the artist has produced a wide range of hues and tones and some fascinating textures.

2 Wash the ink out of the stencil with the appropriate solvent. In this demonstration, oil-based ink is being cleaned off with mineral spirits.

3 When printing from one stencil is complete, it can be cleaned out of the screen mesh. Here, water-based filler is flushed out with a spray jet: the screen stands upright in a custom-built trough. Stubborn traces of filler can be scrubbed with a soft brush.

Cleaning the screen
1 Between each printing, you must clear the screen of ink. Use the squeegee to collect excess ink into a puddle, then pick it up on a palette knife.

TUSCHE METHOD

The method of preparing stencils by the tusche method is similar to the filler method, but there is one crucial difference – this is a resist technique which produces a "positive" stencil. The image is drawn up with tusche (drawing ink) and/or lithographic crayon, both of which are oil-based materials with a greasy texture.

The finished drawing on the screen mesh is coated with gum arabic and left to dry. This acts to block the mesh, as does blue filler, but does not adhere to the tusche. The image is then washed out with mineral spirits, but the gum arabic, being water-soluble, remains in place. The open areas of the stencil are now those marks that you originally drew and painted, so that the printed image is a positive reading of what was first applied.

Using tusche

1 Work directly on the screen with tusche, using any typical painting techniques. This picture shows spattering applied with a toothbrush

between paper masks, after parts of the image have been drawn with a paintbrush.

2 Lithographic crayon can also be used to give a different quality of line. Technically, it acts on the screen mesh in the same way as the tusche. To make the first stencil, you can draw quite freely, or follow a working sketch or painted study if you prefer.

3 Allow the painting on the mesh to dry completely before moving on to the next stage. To save a long wait, you can use a hairdryer to speed up this process.

4 Spread a thin layer of gum arabic over the whole image area. Use a small rectangle of cardboard or plastic to help coat the mesh quickly and evenly. Allow the gum to dry.

5 Wash out the tusche image with mineral spirits applied with a rag or sponge. This has no effect on the gum arabic, so you are left with a gummed stencil consisting of the negative areas of your drawing; therefore the positive marks will print.

Stage proof: one
The first printed image has a fresh, painterly quality with interestingly varied textures. The rough shading of the sea was made by a frottage technique, placing the mesh over a board, then rubbing over it with the litho crayon.

Finished print
Second or subsequent colors can be printed by preparing stencils in the same way, using the original print or your working sketch as a guide. The medium green and pale flesh tint applied here maintain a bright, airy quality appropriate to the subject, while overprinting on the left-hand side introduces an effect of deep shadow.

DRYPOINT

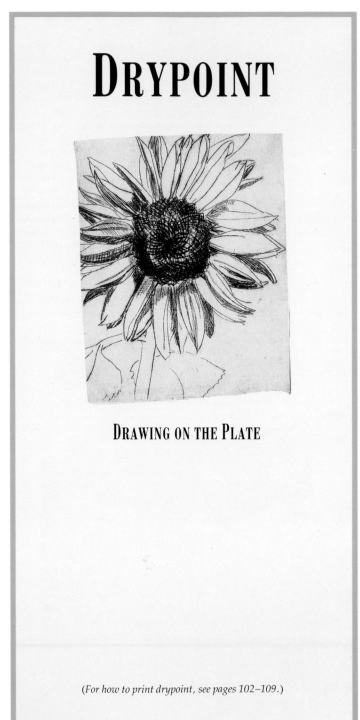

DRAWING ON THE PLATE

(For how to print drypoint, see pages 102–109.)

Because it is the simplest and most direct of the intaglio processes, drypoint is an interesting introduction to working on metal, especially if you have limited access to printmaking facilities. The technique consists of scratching into the surface of a metal plate using a strong, sharp point. The point is used to score the surface, which causes a ridge of metal – called the burr – to be thrown up on one or both sides of the line. This burr holds more ink than

1

2

3

4

DRAWING ON THE PLATE

Any of the effects associated with line drawing can be expressed through drypoint. You can vary line qualities by altering the pressure and angle of the tool, using the point to score or pick at the metal. The burr is raised most consistently by holding the tool upright or at a steep angle; if the point goes in at too shallow an angle there is a danger that it may undercut the burr and lose the richness of the line.

The character of the drawing can rely mainly on outline or contour, but if you want to introduce shaded areas, you can do so by means of conventional drawing techniques such as hatching and crosshatching with close-set parallel lines, or a form of stippling achieved with short, stabbing marks. However, the final state of the print need not depend solely on the positive marks made by the point; you can also use a scraper or burnisher to remove the burr, thus lightening up an area that has been overworked.

the relatively shallow scratches and contributes a velvety, rich quality to the impression.

Drawing on the plate with the point is directly comparable to drawing on paper, though you must use enough pressure to mark the metal effectively. But it is an informal process, immediately accessible to anyone with some drawing ability. Its main disadvantage in comparison with other intaglio printmaking methods is that the burrs wear down quickly under the normal actions of inking the plate and passing it through the press, so the number of good-quality prints that can be taken is limited.

Tools and materials

The only materials needed are a plate and a point. Copper or zinc plates are commonly used. Zinc, being a softer metal, is easier to work, but produces fewer good impressions. For the drawing tool, a hard steel needle or scribe with a smooth, unfaceted point is generally adequate; the alternative is a point made of precious stone such as diamond.

Because of the relative fragility of the drypoint image, working proofs that allow you to check the progress of the drawing must be kept to a minimum. The plate can be prepared without access to any studio facilities; for inking and printing techniques, see the chapter on intaglio printing*.

Drypoint equipment
1 Combined drypoint needle and burnisher; **2** drypoint needle; **3** combined scraper and burnisher; **4** zinc and copper plates.

FURTHER INFORMATION

* Intaglio printing, pages 102–109

1 Start to draw on the plate with the needle as you would with a pencil on paper. It is easiest to sketch out a few faint guidelines first, then gradually strengthen the lines and develop the textures.

2 Changing the angle of the tool enables you to create more or less burr on the line, while more pressure gives you increased thickness. Try to vary the line qualities expressively, according to the details of your subject.

3 You can create grayed areas by hatching blocks of fine parallel lines. The closer the lines and the more burred the marks, the heavier the tonal emphasis will be.

Finished print
The first prints from the finished plate (near left) have a very rich tone, with dense blacks on the darker cat. This is due to the heavy burr created by the stippled marks. After several impressions, you can see how the dark shades have faded (far left) as the burr wears down in printing – individual marks are visible on the cat's back. Altogether ten acceptable prints were pulled from this plate.

4 Once the design is fully drawn out, pull a proof to check the image. In this example (left), the shapes are judged to be satisfactory, but the tones are not yet rich enough.

5 The drawing is worked much more heavily on the plate with hatched and stippled textures. A second proof is pulled (right) as work on the plate nears completion and, using this as a guide, some unwanted lines are smoothed out with the burnisher.

Mezzotint

Rocking the Plate

Scraping and Burnishing

(For how to print mezzotints, see pages 102–109.)

Mezzotint is an unusual intaglio process in two respects. Preparation of the plate requires quite intense physical labor; and the image is worked light out of dark, a reversal of typical approaches in drawing and printmaking. Before any creative work can begin, the plate surface is systematically roughened to produce an overall texture that prints as an even, dense black. Medium shades and whites are retrieved by smoothing out this texture to varying degrees.

The tonal emphasis gives mezzotint prints a soft, often atmospheric quality with minimal linear structure. The technique was invented primarily as a reproduction process that would provide a more painterly effect than line engraving, allowing subtly fluid gradation of tone. It has not been consistently exploited as a creative medium in its own right, and the tedious, purely mechanical aspect of "rocking" the plate to achieve the initial tone can be a deterrent. However, the character of the mezzotint impression is

Mezzotint equipment
1 Coarse mezzotint rocker; **2** fine mezzotint rocker; **3** copper plate; **4** burnisher; **5** curved scraper.

unique, and the transition to pale tones, even high whites, out of intense, rich darks can have great dramatic impact.

Tools and materials
Copper plate is used for mezzotint, and the tool for creating the rough ground is the mezzotint rocker, a broad chisel-like implement with a curved, toothed blade. The

1

2

teeth indent the plate surface and throw up a burr. To achieve a consistent texture, the rocker has to be moved gradually all over the plate in all directions, and a rocking pole is often used to assist the action. Rockers are made in several sizes with teeth differently spaced – fine, closely set teeth give the most

3

consistent tone; a coarse rocker creates more burr and therefore provides the densest blacks, but with a less even texture overall. If you wish to try out the effect of mezzotint without having to do the hard work of preparation, you can obtain pre-rocked plates. These are mechanically prepared, with an even texture, but they are expensive.

The process of "drawing" on the plate – bringing back the lighter tones – involves removing or smoothing down the burr using a scraper and burnisher. To rework an area where you have taken out too much of the tone, you can use a roulette – a small, serrated wheel set in a handle, which can be rolled across the plate to enhance detail or repair the ground. Roulettes are available in different shapes and sizes.

4

5

ROCKING THE PLATE

The reason why rocking the plate is such a laborious process is that it must be done quite consistently in several different directions – first at right angles to the sides of the plate, then along diagonal paths from the edges. The time it takes depends partly on the size of the plate in relation to

the width of the rocker; a very large plate may take days to prepare.

A grid of parallel lines is drawn up to guide the tool, which is held upright on the surface and rocked from side to side on the curved blade, at the same time moving gradually forward along the grid lines. When the rocker is hand-held, the movement comes from the forearm and wrist rather than just the hand. The weighted rocking pole relieves some of the strain of this action by contributing a consistent pressure and keeping the tool on a straight path.

Using the rocker
1 If you are working on a large plate, using a rocking pole helps to lighten the physical effort of rocking the texture initially. The weighted pole can be supported on a frame that allows it to rock easily while keeping a consistent direction, or it can be rested on the work surface.

2 Grasp the pole right behind the point where the rocker is attached and rock it steadily from side to side, at the same time gradually pushing it forward across the plate.

3 You can alternatively rock without the pole, which puts more pressure on your forearm. The plate must be rocked in many different directions to obtain a dense texture, indicated by the grid lines visible here.

SCRAPING AND BURNISHING

Individual or combined processes of scraping and burnishing can be used to develop the variation of tones. The scraper removes the burr, and the burnisher polishes the surface; to work back to pure white, both tools must be used. Intermediate grays can be formed by scraping and burnishing to different degrees or just by using the burnisher gently to flatten the burr. The only way of finding out the extent and degree of either action required for a particular effect is through experience.

To give yourself a layout for the design, you can start by drawing on the roughened plate with a soft pencil. You can also rub ink into the plate so that you are working on a black surface, which helps you to estimate the effect of the scraping and burnishing. If you do this, clean off the ink each time you stop work, or it will dry hard and you may damage the burr of the plate while trying to remove it. Keep proofing to a minimum, as the printing process gradually wears down the texture. For printing mezzotints, see the chapter on intaglio printing*.

FURTHER INFORMATION

*Intaglio printing: pages 102–109

Drawing on the plate
1 Guidelines for the design can be drawn on the metal using a soft pencil. Where a sharp outline is needed, draw into the rocked texture with a metal scribe.

2 The curved tip of a burnisher flattens the burr on the metal plate. The shaded area will print as a light tone, graduating to dark as it recedes from the outline.

3 You can work with a scraper to clear very pale-toned areas quickly. This has a less delicate effect than a burnisher: it is a matter of personal preference which to use, according to the character of the design.

Philip Coombs
Doll's Head (Mezzotint)
The graded tones of mezzotint have an almost photographic quality when applied to heavily modeled shapes. The strong black of the fully rocked texture, as seen in the background of this image, has a rich, velvety intensity.

ETCHING

PREPARING THE PLATE

APPLYING HARD GROUND

DRAWING ON THE PLATE

BITING THE PLATE

AQUATINT

SOFT-GROUND ETCHING

SUGAR-LIFT PROCESS

ETCHED TEXTURES

(For how to print etchings, see pages 102–109.)

The essential difference between etching techniques and the other intaglio methods is that the marks are not achieved by incising or scraping the metal. The image is developed by corroding the metal plate with acid, using acid-resistant grounds to protect the areas not to be etched.

The variety of materials and techniques that can be applied to etching makes it a remarkably versatile and expressive area of printmaking. Different ways of manipulating the grounds, the mark-making processes, the action and extent of the corrosion, and the printing process give the artist an infinite range of creative opportunities.

Tools and materials

To produce even the most basic etched impression, you will need quite a wide range of materials and equipment, and it is essential to learn the techniques under supervision in a properly equipped studio. Safety factors are particularly important. At various stages

Etching equipment
1 Hard ground; **2** soft ground; **3** stopping-out varnish; **4** liquid hard ground; **5** zinc and copper plates; **6** leather-covered dabber; **7** burnisher; **8** etching needle; **9** scraper; **10** feathers for clearing acid bubbles from plate; **11** clamp for holding plate during smoking.

the plate has to be heated on a hotplate or burner, and the process of etching involves using an acid bath which should be placed well away from other work areas and must be well-ventilated to remove fumes. It is not advisable to consider setting up an etching studio at home until you are confident of the techniques, and even then it can be difficult to arrange.

The simplest assortment of etching equipment consists of a metal plate, acid-resistant

3

4

5

7

8

9

ground and varnish, an etching needle, and an acid bath. Copper or zinc plates are usually chosen, although steel and other metals are also suitable. Copper provides more refined effects of line and tone and, being harder, stands up better to the wear and tear of inking and printing. But zinc (or a zinc-like alloy offered by some suppliers) is a perfectly adequate and less expensive material on which to learn the craft.

Etching grounds are either hard or soft. The hard ground is the standard one for line etching, while the soft ground* creates different, particular surface effects. Both are available in solid cake form and are melted onto the plate and spread with a dabber or roller. Alternatively, a liquid hard ground can be used. Stopping-out varnish is an acid-resistant liquid applied to reinforce the ground in areas not to be etched – or to cover up exposed metal.

The etching needle is a smooth, lightweight metal point. It should not be too sharp, as it is important that it does not scratch the metal as you draw into the ground. It is advisable to obtain a custom-made tool, but you can improvise with a darning needle attached firmly to a pen or brush handle. The type and strength of acid solution, or mordant, depends on the metal being used and the intensity of the corrosive effect* required.

Further materials and equipment are needed for the aquatint process* and for printing the plate, but the basic method of printing* for all intaglio images is the same. If you use a professionally equipped etching studio, either rented commercially or as part of an educational institution, it will have all the facilities you need for any of the techniques described here.

FURTHER INFORMATION

* Biting the plate, pages 92–93
* Aquatint, pages 94–95
* Soft ground etching, pages 96–97
* Intaglio printing, pages 102–109

6

10

11

PREPARING THE PLATE

The intaglio (sunken) areas of an etching plate can be quite deep, in some cases both deep and narrow, and so the print has to be pulled under heavy pressure. Because the paper is forced into the sunken areas, it becomes embossed to some extent, as well as picking up the ink. If the plate has hard, vertical edges, these can cut through the paper under pressure, even though the thickness of the metal is no more than $\frac{1}{16}$–$\frac{1}{8}$ inch. To avoid damage to the paper and the soft blankets that help to spread the pressure of the press rollers, the edges of the plate are beveled to an angle of about 45 degrees by rubbing them down with a file. This is usually done as a preliminary process, although edges can also be filed and polished immediately before printing.

Before laying the acid-resistant ground, the surface must be clean and completely free of grease; otherwise, the ground may adhere imperfectly and cause the effect known as "foul-biting" in the acid, when blemishes allow non-printing areas of the plate to become mildly and irregularly corroded.

Beveling the plate
1 Position the plate so that it is firmly supported but one edge just protrudes from the edge of the work surface. File all along the edge, keeping the file at an angle of 45 degrees. Repeat on all sides of the plate.

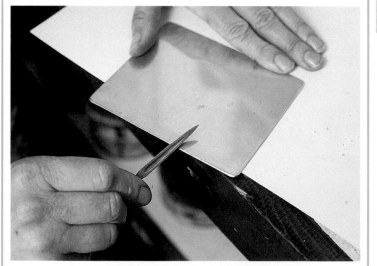

2 To smooth any marks that the file has left, you can work along the beveled edges with a scraper, held at the same angle. Shave the metal lightly with the scraper blade.

3 You can leave mitered corners or, if you prefer, round them off completely. Because intaglio prints have a slightly embossed effect, the edges of the plate do leave a clear impression on the paper, so they should be even and clean.

Degreasing

1 Put a small heap of talc or whiting on the plate and pour in a few drops of household ammonia.

2 Work the ammonia and talc into a paste and rub it across the whole plate surface, using a lightweight scrubbing brush, absorbent cotton, or a soft rag.

3 Rinse the plate with clean water. If it is completely degreased, the water will flow evenly across the surface. If the water runs around remaining grease spots, repeat the process. Then dry the plate.

APPLYING HARD GROUND

The ground must be applied evenly to form an effective acid-resistant coating that is durable but can be lifted easily and cleanly as you draw into it with the etching needle. The solid ball of hard ground that you buy from the supplier is shiny and brownish-black. The basic ingredients are bitumen, wax, and rosin (colophony), but there are various recipes, and some etchers prefer to make their own. It is applied to a warmed plate, heated gently on a hotplate. Dabs of ground melt onto the surface of the metal and are rolled out in all directions to form a smooth, thin coating. The completed ground is a warm, golden-brown color.

It is important not to "overcook" the ground, as too much heat causes it first to slide on the surface, then to coagulate and stick to the applicator so that the coating becomes lumpy and uneven. If this happens, cool the plate, clean it off, and start again. Getting the right touch in grounding a plate is a matter of practice; for instance, you may find a forward pass of the roller lays down the coating, and a quick backward roll lifts any excess.

Smoking
Smoking the ground with wax tapers, which hardens it slightly and turns it a darker color, is not essential, but it does make it easier to see the marks of your drawing with the needle. Wax tapers which give off a dark smoke that deposits carbon on the ground are used. Only the smoky trail from the wax tapers, not the naked flame, should touch the ground, which turns black and shiny as it carbonizes. Using the center of the flame can scorch the ground, and it will begin to flake.

Applying hard ground
1 Put the degreased plate on the hotplate and let it warm up. Dab the ball of hard ground onto the surface, allowing it to melt into random smears.

2 Use a hard-wearing roller to spread the ground evenly across the plate, working in all directions.

3 Continue to work with the roller, traveling from side to side both ways on the plate until the ground is thin and even, and a uniform golden-brown color.

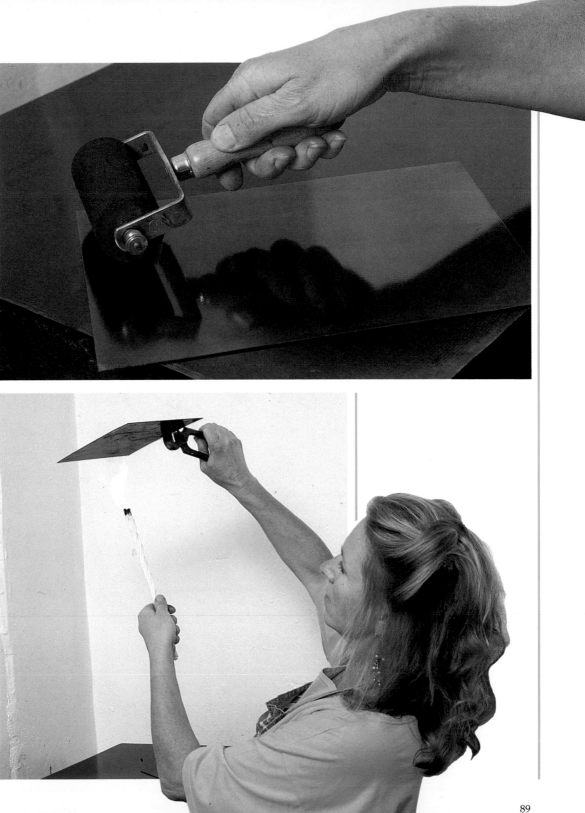

Smoking the ground
Secure the plate at one edge in a pair of pliers or hand-held clamp. Put a small fold of paper at the edge to prevent the tool from marking the plate surface. Light three or four wax tapers twisted together to make a long flame. Move the flame under the plate in a circling motion, so that only the smoke trail from the wax tapers touches the ground. Continue until the ground darkens all over.

DRAWING ON THE PLATE

Once the ground has been smoked and allowed to cool, you are ready to start drawing. If you wish to put down guidelines, you can draw on the ground with a soft, blunted pencil or trace your design using transfer paper. However, the point of any print process is to exploit the characteristics of the materials and methods, so don't try to copy a preparatory drawing too slavishly – let the composition evolve freely on the plate.

You can manipulate the etching needle in just the same ways that you would a pencil or pen. The important thing to remember is that it need only lift the ground – it is actually a disadvantage if it scratches into the metal – so do not apply too much pressure. The work of cutting into the metal is all done by the acid, and if your lines are unevenly scored into the plate, this will affect the quality of the acid bite. You do need to expose the plate cleanly, however; if you can still see a thin brown film across the line, the ground is not fully removed.

You will gradually get used to the effects of etching and learn the best ways to draw your image. A very broad line will bite as a shallow furrow in the metal, and because of the surface quality of the intaglio and the method of inking and wiping the plate for printing, it will print paler at the center than at the edges. In hatched areas where lines are close together, the acid may break through the tiny sections of ground dividing them. If you wish to begin with fairly even, black line work, keep the drawing relatively fine and the textures clean and distinct.

Stopping out

Before etching, every part of the plate surface that is not deliberately exposed as part of the image to be etched must be completely protected by an acid-resistant covering. This involves painting the back and the bevelled edges of the plate with stopping-out varnish – the plate may have been supplied with a prepared acid-resist backing, but the edges must still be stopped out.

On the front of the plate, any part of the ground where there is no drawing can be covered with varnish to prevent foul-biting. You can also use stopping-out varnish to refine lines scratched too coarsely in the ground or to cover errors.

Drawing on the plate
1 If you are transferring an existing design to the plate, cover it with transfer or carbon paper and lay a tracing of your drawing on top.

2 Tape the one edge of the tracing so that it is anchored in position. Go over the drawing with a pencil so the transfer paper lays down the lines on the ground beneath.

3 Draw directly into the ground with an etching needle as freely as you would draw on paper with a pencil. Avoid scratching into the surface of the metal. The lines you make should just lift the ground cleanly.

Alternative tools
1 You can use other implements to work into the ground. An ordinary ink pen makes calligraphic, double lines because of the split in the nib.

2 A small roulette – this is a dentist's drill bit – rolled over the ground makes a lightly toothed linear pattern.

Stopping out
When the drawing on the ground is complete, paint stopping-out varnish over any non-printing areas where the ground is imperfect. Finally, stop out the edges and back of the plate as necessary, so no bare metal will be exposed to the acid except in the drawing.

BITING THE PLATE

The action of acid on metal is called the "bite." One of the difficulties for the beginner is that there are no simple rules for estimating how long the plate needs to be in the acid bath. The speed and strength of the bite varies according to a number of factors – the types of metal and acid used, the extent of plate surface exposed to acid, the temperature of the acid bath and that of the studio environment. You also have to consider the effect you wish to achieve – whether the lines should be fine and shallow-bitten, or deep and strong. This is all learned by experience, but even so it remains a relatively unpredictable technique.

A plate can be bitten in stages to produce different line qualities. All the lines are bitten for a certain length of time, then the plate is removed from the acid, rinsed and dried, the fine lines are covered with stopping-out varnish, and the plate is returned to the acid to etch the remaining lines more deeply. A detailed image may require many different stages of grounding and biting. It is difficult, though not impossible, to rework bitten lines cleanly through a new ground. The addition of shading and texture may, however, alter the effect of the initial line work, and decisions about reworking can be made on the basis of proofs pulled at different stages.

The acid bath

The container for the acid solution can be a glass, porcelain or plastic dish or tray – obviously the material must not be susceptible to the corrosive effect. Ideally, it should be sited under an extractor fan; at the least it must stand in a well-ventilated part of the studio. When checking a plate in the acid, do not stand over the bath for too long, because you will be breathing in fumes.

It is essential to work carefully and steadily when handling acid bottles and mixing solutions. Preferably this will be done for you by an experienced teacher or technician. Acid and water generate heat when combined, so to control this, the acid must be added to the water, never vice versa. The solution for the acid bath, which varies from a 1:1 ratio to about 10:1 water to acid, depending upon the purpose, is safer to work with than full-strength acid, but you should still take precautions like wearing rubber gloves, and if any of the solution splashes on your skin, rinse it off with clean water.

For copper and zinc plates, nitric acid can be used. The solution is made slightly stronger for copper, which bites slowly, and the acid gradually turns blue as it acts on the metal. On zinc, the acid bites quite quickly and produces bubbles on the plate surface. These must be removed with a soft brush or feather; otherwise, the bubbles form a sort of acid-resist and the result is a textured bite.

Two other solutions commonly used are Dutch mordant for copper – a mixture of hydrochloric acid, potassium chlorate, and water – and ferric chloride, used for copper or zinc. Be sure to get professional advice on the type of mordant to use and its strength for the job in hand.

Biting the plate
1 Lower the plate gently into the acid bath. In the parts of this process when your fingers are likely to be in contact with the acid, it is wise to wear rubber gloves.

2 As the acid begins to act on the metal, you will see bubbles forming on the plate. Brush them away gently with a feather.

3 When the biting is complete, remove the plate from the acid, transfer it to the sink, and wash it with clean running water.

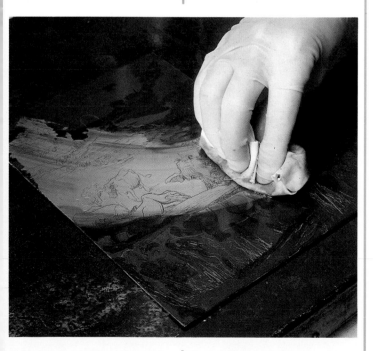

4 Return the plate to the work surface and wipe off the ground and stopping-out varnish with mineral spirits. When the plate is completely clean, you are ready to take a first-stage proof.

5 A line etching reflects the vitality of your drawing and at the same time contributes qualities of its own – particularly the richness of the black line, due to the amount of ink held in the intaglio. You can produce finished etchings in line work only. This example will be given more overall shading with the addition of aquatint (see overleaf).

AQUATINT

This process enables you to create both areas of solid tone on an etching plate and gradations of tone from white through a range of grays to black. It is commonly combined with line etching to give weight and modeling to the image, but can be used as the primary technique.

Aquatint involves laying a coating of resin dust on the plate, which is then heated, causing the resin to melt into tiny globules. On removal from the heat, these harden, and when the plate is etched, the acid eats into the pits between the globules to produce a fine, all-over intaglio texture. Tonal variations are made by successive stages of stopping out areas of the plate and biting the exposed shapes in the acid, gradually etching the pitted surface more deeply. To check the tones, the resin must be removed with solvent before proofing the plate, so you cannot rebite into the same texture after proofing.

Areas which are too dark can be retrieved by burnishing, although this affects the texture. You can also use aquatint as a dark-to-light method, like mezzotint, by biting a continuous dark tone over the whole plate and working into it with a scraper and burnisher.

Applying aquatint resin

There are several ways of doing this, and the choice will depend on the facilities available and the textural effect you wish to produce. A dense, even aquatint tone is best achieved by using a custom-built aquatint box. This is fitted with bellows or a revolving paddle worked from outside, with which you agitate the resin dust in the box so that it flies up in a dense cloud. The plate is then inserted face up and the dust allowed to settle.

The alternative is to apply the resin direct to the plate with some kind of shaker. Various devices can be used – a cheesecloth bag; a salt shaker; a jar with cheesecloth stretched across the top; a fine sifter. The more random and uncontrollable the fall of resin from the shaker, the more irregular the aquatint texture.

A rough aquatint can be

Applying aquatint resin
1 The easiest and most reliable way to apply aquatint is in a custom-built box, fitted with a revolving paddle. The box contains a large amount of resin which, when the box is not in use, settles in the bottom of the drum (see diagram).

effective in prints that incorporate textural variety, but if you are looking for subtle tonal gradations, the resin must be finely and evenly laid.

Biting an aquatint

Appreciable variations of tone occur in minutes, even seconds, as you go through successive bitings. At the first stage, you stop out* the areas of the plate to remain white, and also cover the back and edges of the plate with varnish. The acid solution should not be too strong, or it may eat sideways under the resin rather than etching down evenly into the pitted texture. After the first biting, remove the plate from the acid, rinse and dry it. Then stop out the next lightest shade and return the plate briefly to the acid.

This process is continued until you have as many shades as you require. The accumulated time that the plate is in the acid may be less than an hour overall, but you need time in between for stopping out. The varnish must cover the aquatint grain thickly and cleanly and be allowed to dry completely before the plate is rebitten. Be careful not to leave the plate too long in the acid on the final bite, or it may break down the resin ground, resulting in a foul-bitten, irregular texture.

If you have begun with line etching, your line work will provide a guide for laying in the aquatint tones. If you are working directly on the aquatint ground, you can trace a layout using transfer paper.

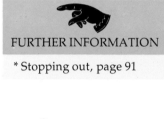

FURTHER INFORMATION

* Stopping out, page 91

A: stirring up resin dust

B: inserting etching plate   C: allowing dust to settle

2 Close up the front of the box and turn the handle vigorously. This turns the paddle which agitates the resin dust and causes it to fly up inside the drum (see diagram A).

3 Lock the handle in the position where it keeps the interior paddle horizontal. Put your etching plate on a wire tray and insert it in the box. A face mask prevents you from inhaling any dust that drifts out. Close up the front of the box again (see diagram B).

4 After a few minutes, check that an even coating of resin has fallen onto the plate (see diagram C), then remove the plate from the tray and transfer it to a metal grid. Use a small blowtorch or Bunsen burner to heat the plate from underneath.

5 Keep the heat source moving gently underneath the plate so that it does not scorch the resin. The whitish, powdery coating gradually melts and turns yellow. When this color has spread right across the plate, allow it to cool.

Aquatint tones

You can stop out areas of the design and return the plate to the acid several times to produce a range of tones, but overbiting may break down the aquatint. In this example, there are three grays — pale, medium, and dark, and the heavier black. Pale gray might require only seconds in the acid, black several minutes in all. The tonal modeling can considerably alter the character of the print — compare this version with the line etching on page 93.

SOFT-GROUND ETCHING

Soft ground is similar in composition to hard ground, but it has a higher grease content that contributes the softer texture. It is applied to the plate in the same way as hard ground*, using a roller or dauber to spread the coating evenly and thinly. A soft ground is not smoked.

You can draw directly into soft ground with an etching needle to produce a line drawing with a softer, less precise character than that typical of work on hard ground. However, where soft ground really comes into its own is in using techniques that depend upon making an impression in the ground. Because the coating is soft and tacky, it is picked up by any material pressed down hard against it. You can draw through a piece of paper onto the ground to produce a line resembling soft pencil or crayon marks. All sorts of materials leave a clear impression that etches quite accurately – woven fabrics, yarns and meshes, feathers, thin wood-grain. To make the impression, the material is laid on the plate, covered with a clean sheet of paper and rolled through the press.

FURTHER INFORMATION

* Applying hard ground, pages 88–89

2 Use a hard but not sharp point to impress on the paper. Here the artist is working with a plastic knitting needle.

3 At any stage of the drawing you can lift the paper to check the impression on the plate, but be sure to keep one side of the paper firmly anchored, so it goes back down in exactly the same place.

Soft-ground textures
1 To make a drawing on soft ground, either work direct onto a clean piece of paper laid over the plate, or make a master drawing beforehand that you can trace over.

4 When using "found" materials to create soft-ground textures, simply lay the pieces on the plate in the appropriate position.

8 Stop out any non-printing areas of the plate and protect the back and edges as necessary. You can now etch the plate in acid – keep checking the action of the acid bite, so that fragile textures do not break down.

5 It is worth experimenting with all kinds of materials – some textures "take" better than others. This example shows tracing paper, tarlatan, cellophane, string, ribbon, batting, and dried leaves from the onions that are the subject of the print.

6 Move the plate to the bed of the press and cover it with a clean sheet of paper. Run it through the press so that the pressure embeds the materials firmly in the ground.

7 Lift the materials from the plate very carefully, without actually touching the ground. You can pick up paper or fibrous materials with an etching needle, or catch one end with tweezers.

9 The final result of this print is a very pleasing combination of tones and textures. Although the materials were quite randomly chosen, they suit the subject well, and the contrast of soft lines and tonal masses gives the image weight and depth.

SUGAR-LIFT PROCESS

This process is generally associated with aquatint, but can also be used to expose areas of the plate for open biting. (This term simply means exposing a broad area of the plate surface to acid, as compared to line work or the grainy texture of aquatint.) Usually, when you use stopping-out varnish to protect unexposed areas, you are painting it on as a negative surround to the shapes that will be bitten. The sugar-lift process is a resist technique that enables you to etch any shape that you have painted positively, from a solid, flat area to a textured brushmark.

You paint your design on the plate with a sugar solution colored with ink or gouache, allow it to dry, and cover it with diluted stopping-out varnish or liquid hard ground. You then immerse the plate in warm water, and the sugar gradually dissolves and lifts the varnish, leaving the acid-resistant coating in place around the painted marks. You can then aquatint the exposed areas or etch them as they are.

Sugar-lift process
1 Paint your design with the sugar solution on a clean, degreased plate. The solution used here was one part sugar to four parts water and one part ink. Heat the water to dissolve the sugar grains.

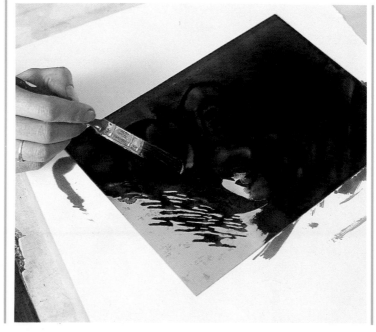

2 Allow the sugar painting to dry completely – this can take some time, especially if the atmosphere is humid, as the sugar re-absorbs moisture. When dry, cover the whole plate with a thin coat of stopping-out varnish diluted with mineral spirits.

3 When the stopping-out varnish has dried, immerse the plate in a bath of water. Leave it until the sugar begins to dissolve and the varnish lifts.

Then you can brush it lightly to assist the process.

4 When the sugar coating has all lifted, leaving the design exposed in the varnish layer, place it in acid to bite as required (you can apply aquatint over the varnish if preferred). This plate is open biting – the bubbles show the fast action of the acid on the exposed metal.

5 The resist technique retains the fluid, calligraphic quality of the original painting. Open biting typically produces the strong outlines visible in this print, especially if the plate is etched quite deeply. After the first bite, parts of the image were stopped out and the plate returned to the acid for further biting, which produced the darker shades in the outlines and small shapes.

ETCHED TEXTURES

Etching provides a far greater variety of surface effects than any other intaglio process. All the techniques previously described can be combined on one plate, and there is plenty of room to experiment. For example, stopping-out varnish floated onto water breaks up into fascinating marbled textures that can be transferred to the metal simply by holding the plate face down on the water surface. There are also many variations that can be obtained using different materials to impress a soft ground, or by applying stopping-out varnish to a clean plate using standard painting techniques such as dry brushing and spattering. The strength and depth of the acid bite can also be exploited to vary shading and detail.

You need to plan carefully so that your composition does not become overloaded with busy textures, but since the marks that result from different processes are all etched into a single surface, they generally cohere very well when printed.

Marbling
Stopping-out varnish floated on water picks up on the surface of the plate and etches into this rich, random pattern. The striped effect is caused by open biting between strips painted with stopping-out varnish. The white areas represent the unetched plate surface.

Drawing and impressing
The lines were drawn in the hard ground with free, quick strokes of the etching needle. The rounded smudges are fingerprints, made by pressing on the ground with a fingertip dampened with mineral spirits.

Rough open bite
This fully exposed area of the plate was left in the acid for a long period. The bubbles building up on the metal due to the action of the acid gradually formed a resist; the bite worked around the bubbles to produce this pebbly texture.

Combined textures
The grid is composed of lines ruled in hard ground, the smoother tonal areas are shallow open biting applied to areas exposed by wiping the ground with mineral spirits on a rag. The scumbled texture was rubbed into the ground with steel wool. The "bird's wing" detail was made by drybrushing into the ground with a brush dipped in mineral spirits; the resulting marks were allowed to etch a long time without feathering.

Open bite and aquatint
The spotted pattern was formed by spattering mineral spirits onto hard ground and blotting with a rag. The dark background is aquatint, the orange colour a coating of ink rolled over the plate surface.

Soft ground and aquatint
The wood-grain effect was achieved by impressing a thin wood veneer into soft ground. The crisscross wire pattern was fully stopped out while the wood texture was etched and was later aquatinted to achieve the tonal variations.

Etching and drypoint
Various areas of etched open bite and linear textures produced an interestingly atmospheric print, but lacked strong contrast. The darkest shade was supplied by raising a burr with a drypoint needle on the zinc plate.

INTAGLIO PRINTING

PREPARING THE PAPER

INKING AND WIPING

PULLING THE PRINT

COLOR PRINTING

(This chapter shows how to print the intaglio methods of drypoint, mezzotint and etching.)

The method of printing from an intaglio plate is essentially the same for all processes – drypoint, engraving, mezzotint, and etching. Unlike block printing or lithography, when it is strictly surface contact that forms the impression, the pressure of printing must force the paper into the intaglio to pick up an even impression from marks as varied as fine creviced lines, delicate aquatinting, and deep, open bite. The way the paper is pushed into the lines and sunken areas in the plate produces an embossed effect that adds an extra dimension to the print.

A flat-bed press is used, consisting of a heavy metal bed that passes between two large rollers. Studio presses are usually very heavy and work on a gearing system that makes it easier to move the weight of the bed, operated by turning a large wheel at one side. The space between the rollers can be varied to alter the pressure. Soft felt blankets, which cushion the rollers and spread the pressure evenly, are used to cover the plate and bed before they are pressed through the rollers.

Equipment for intaglio printing
1 Glass mixing slab; **2** tube intaglio ink; **3** palette knife; **4** coarse and fine tarlatan; **5** intaglio ink; **6** powder pigment; **7** plate oil; **8** blotting paper and tissue; **9** rollers.

PREPARING PAPER

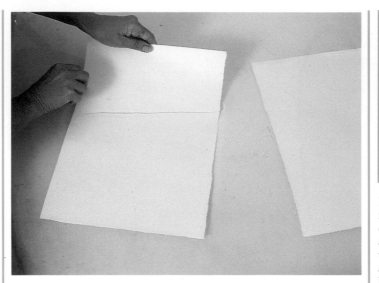

Intaglio plates are printed on damp paper, which gives more flexibility for pressing into the intaglio without the paper splitting or failing to pick up all the ink. The paper is prepared beforehand by soaking in clean water. It is then drained and blotted, interleaved with blotting paper, pressed between boards, and left until needed.

High-quality watercolor papers are often chosen for intaglio printing, particularly handmade or mold-made papers with deckle edges which look good when framed without a mat. It is important that the weight and texture of the paper suits the style and complexity of the image, so that fine marks are picked up accurately where appropriate and the qualities of the print do not compete with that of the printing surface.

Preparing paper
1 Put the paper to soak in a bath of clean water. The amount of time it needs to soak depends on the weight and texture of the paper – it must become fully damp right through the fibers.

2 Lift the paper from the water bath and let it drain. Lay it on a sheet of blotting paper and cover it with a second sheet. You can build up a stack of paper layers in this way. Lay a board on top to press it so the paper sheets remain flat and moist.

INKING AND WIPING

Before you start to pull a print, make sure the plate is completely clean and free of any traces of ground or varnish. Check that the edges are cleanly bevelled; if they have been damaged during the etching process, file them smooth again.

The inking process requires a heavy first application of ink, which must be rubbed well into the plate so that it is pushed into all the intaglio marks. The plate is then wiped carefully and thoroughly to take off all surplus color. This is easiest to do if the plate is warmed slightly on a hotplate, but heating is not always essential. It is important that there is no "loose" ink left on the surface after wiping, as this will prevent the true shading of the intaglio from being seen, and make it impossible to produce identical prints.

Although ready-mixed inks are available, many printmakers like to mix inks from powder pigments and plate oil. Selecting particular types of pigments, even different kinds of black, gives them control over the tones and colors of the print as well as the consistency of the ink, which can vary from a rich liquid to a thick paste.

The ink can be applied with

a ready-made dauber or simply with a pad of coarse cheesecloth, called tarlatan. The same tartalan is used for wiping, with a slightly finer fabric sometimes chosen for later stages. The final wipe, which polishes the white areas and cleans the pale tones, is done with the heel of the hand, dusted with talc, or with pieces of tissue rubbed flatly over the metal surface. Drypoint plates are not hand-wiped, because the burred texture is abrasive.

Mixing ink

1 Use a broad palette knife to place a heap of powder pigment on the mixing slab. Make a depression in the center and pour in a small pool of plate oil.

2 Push the pigment into the oil from all sides and start to work it into a paste, alternately pressing and lifting the mixture with the knife. Continue until the ink has a smooth consistency. The amount of oil you add determines whether it is stiff or fluid.

Inking the plate

1 Let the clean etching plate warm on the hotplate. Twist a small piece of felt to make a dauber – a firm little pad with a handle that you can hold it by. Pick up ink on the pad and dab it onto the plate.

2 Work the ink into the intaglio all over the plate surface. Use a generous amount of color, and push it firmly into any deep lines and heavily bitten areas.

3 Fold a large piece of tarlatan into a pad and briskly wipe the surface to remove excess ink. Keep the pad traveling flatly across the plate to clean the smoother textures and lighter tones – do not dig the ink out of the deep intaglio.

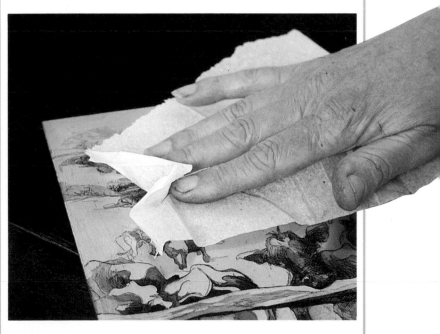

4 When you can see the design clearly, continue wiping with a clean tarlatan, working lightly and consistently so no obvious smears of ink are left on the surface.

To polish the light tones and obtain a clean tonal range from the aquatint areas, go over the plate with a facial tissue. Spread your fingers flat on the tissue and rub with a circular motion.

PULLING THE PRINT

This process is very simple. The plate is positioned on the flat bed of the press and the damp paper laid over the top. The felt blankets are spread over them, between two and five layers, with lightweight felt next to the plate and a heavy, napped blanket next to the press roller. The handle of the press is turned to run the bed between the rollers.

To make sure that the impression is taken square on the paper, with even borders, you can lay a base sheet of paper on the bed of the press with the outline of the plate marked on it. When the printing paper is placed on the plate, the edges can be aligned to the base sheet, working from one corner. Alternatively, you can position masking-tape guides for both plate and paper on the bed of the press.

Taking a print
1 Make sure the blankets are in place on the press, fed in under the roller, but turned back so the bed of the press is clear. Lay the inked plate on a clean sheet of paper on the bed.

2 Turn back the board on the paper stack and lift out one sheet of damp paper. To keep the edges clean, hold it between small paper folds.

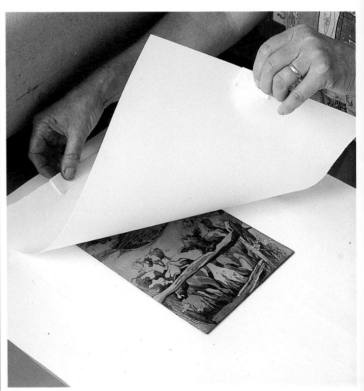

3 Position one corner of the paper on the press in relation to the inked plate. Gently lower the paper and smooth it down on the plate.

4 Pull the blankets down onto the bed of the press one by one, smoothing them carefully in place over the plate and paper.

5 Turn the handle of the press to pass the bed between the rollers. It should turn easily, though a slightly greater effort is required as the thickness of the plate moves through, as the pressure of the rollers does need to be quite heavy.

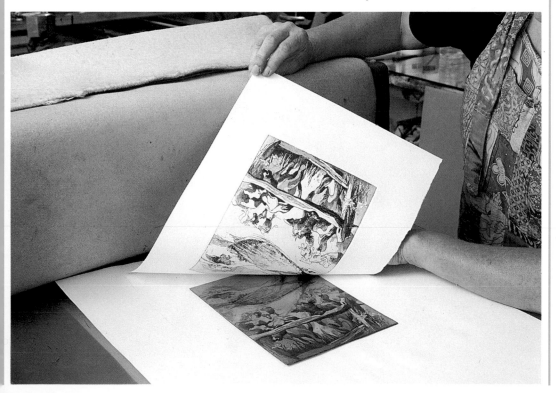

6 Take the bed through far enough to release both the plate and printing paper from beneath the rollers. Turn back the blankets and peel the print up gently from one corner. The finished print is the example shown in full on page 95.

COLOR PRINTING

There are several ways of introducing color into an etching, even when you are working on only one plate. One method is to ink up the intaglio in one color, usually black or a dark color such as blue or sepia, then use a roller to lay down a flat coating of a second color over the plate surface. Any areas required to print white can be masked off with paper before the color roll-up.

You can also ink the intaglio in more than one color, using separate daubers for different parts of the plate. This is not absolutely precise, as color areas will merge or overlap slightly in the process of inking and wiping, but it can produce very expressive and atmospheric results.

A more laborious method, which keeps color areas quite separate, involves cutting up the plate and inking each piece individually. When you print, the pieces are reassembled like a jigsaw puzzle on the bed of the press. The disadvantage is that you are likely to see white lines between the cut pieces on the final impression.

Alternatively, you can overprint separate plates, etched with different parts of the design and inked in different colors. This approach needs careful planning, and you have to register the images accurately, both when preparing the plates and when printing.

Inking in two colors
1 Warm the clean plate on the hotplate. Make a clean dauber out of a tarlatan and apply your first color to the appropriate areas. Wipe off the excess.

2 Apply the second color to the required areas of the plate and wipe off the excess. Wipe again with clean tarlatan, then finish with tissue as before.

3 You cannot get hard edges to the color areas working this way, but both colors appear distinctly, with a gentle transition of mixed tone between them.

Philip Coombs
Window (mezzotint)
This mezzotint image was printed from two plates in separate colors, overprinting one on another. The first plate was light-toned, printed in alizarin crimson; the second, with the image scraped but not burnished into the plate's rocked texture, was inked in Prussian blue and superimposed. The result is a very subtle merging of the two colors, enhancing the atmospheric character of the print and contributing warm lights.

Judy Martin
Jaguar Turning (etching)
The "duotone" effect of this print comes from inking up the intaglio in black, then rolling over the whole surface with orange. As some of the black ink is picked up on the roller, the color has to be laid in one pass with a roller large enough to cover the entire width of the plate. The bars (detail below) are deep-bitten intaglio burnished down the center; the irregular white shapes on the animal's body were formed by laying torn paper masks on the plate before the color roll-up.

LITHOGRAPHY

PREPARING THE PLATE

PROCESSING THE IMAGE

PRINTING

8

Lithography is in one respect an ideal introduction to printmaking because the image is created by standard drawing and painting techniques, put onto the printing surface in exactly the same way as drawing or painting on paper. You describe the image positively, and the marks you make hold the ink for printing. Monochrome lithographs are comparable in tone and texture to crayon or ink line-and-wash drawings. Color lithography involves preparing an individual plate for each color to be printed, but you can build up beautifully wide-ranging effects of surface texture and color by overprinting.

The process depends on a simple chemical principle – the mutual antipathy of oil and water. The image is drawn with greasy materials on a grease-sensitive surface, with the non-printing areas treated with water-based materials to keep them clean. When printing ink is rolled on, it adheres only to the sensitized, greasy marks. The inked image can be printed on paper either by direct contact or by offsetting, that is, taking up the ink from the plate onto an intermediary surface and laying

2

3

1

it down separately on the paper.

Although lithography is such an expressive, painterly medium, the chemical processing can seem initially tedious and difficult to grasp. However, it is carried out in simple stages, all designed to "set" the image on the lithographic plate.

Tools and materials
Originally, lithographic images were prepared on large blocks of limestone and printed by direct contact. This method is still practiced, but it is now more common to use metal plates – zinc or aluminum, depending on which is more easily available. Metal plates can also be printed direct, but are particularly adapted to offset printing. The stone or plate has an even grain which contributes to the characteristic textures of lithographic printing. After printing the surface can be cleaned and resensitized to be used again, but after a few uses it must be completely regrained. There are specialist services for this.

For drawing the image, you can use litho crayons and pencils, and lithographic ink (tusche), brushed on full-strength or as diluted washes. All these materials are black, but once you have drawn and processed the plate, the image can be inked up in any color for printing.

The plate is treated with a number of chemicals in the processing stages. The undrawn plate is first sensitized with a liquid preparation known as "counter-etch." Gum arabic is used to protect non-printing areas while you draw on the plate or to seal the plate surface between stages of processing and printing. The image is "fixed" on the plate by applying a caustic etch solution, such as dilute acid mixed with gum. The term "etch" is confusing if you are already familiar with the physical process of etching* on metal – in lithography, the etch solution does not eat into the plate surface; it simply helps to set the greasy marks.

At all stages of processing and printing, the plate is frequently dampened and dried off. Sponges are common equipment for lithography, and a hairdryer or fan is essential for drying stages – unless you are prepared to wait hours, or even days, to move on to the next step.

Lithography is essentially a studio-based process, so if you attend a class or work in a commercial studio under supervision, you will find most of what you need already available; ask the teacher or technician whether you are expected to supply any of the materials yourself.

Lithography equipment
1 Lithographic stick or liquid tusche;
2 lithographic crayons;
3 pencil and graphite sticks;
4 autographic ink;
5 printing ink;
6 large inking roller; **7** zinc litho plate; **8** pure cellulose sponge.

FURTHER INFORMATION

* Etching, pages 84–101

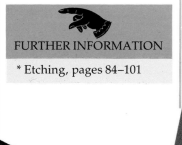

Test plate

Many studios keep printed test sheets that demonstrate various textures you can obtain by using a variety of techniques to draw on the plate with lithographic ink and crayon. Other studio materials that leave a greasy residue on the plate can also be used. The examples shown here are: **1** crayon lines; **2** pen and ink lines; **3** crayon dragged on its side on a textured surface; **4** a solid wash of undiluted litho ink; **5** lithographic pencil lines; **6** wax pencil lines; **7** a wash made with ink floated in water and turpentine; **8** tap-water ink wash; **9** gum arabic resist under oil-based tusche; **10** turpentine wash drawn into with ink; **11** sponged ink; **12** spattered ink; **13** spray paint.

PREPARING THE PLATE

There are a few minor variations possible in the steps and materials applied to preparing and processing a lithographic plate. The demonstration sequence shown here describes a standard series of stages, which explains the basic principles and practice, but you may be taught a slightly different method at the studio where you work.

Initially, once the plate surfaces have been prepared, the artist draws and paints on as many plates as are required for the number of colors to print. A working drawing helps you to identify which details to include on the plate for each color. To lay out the guidelines of your composition, you can sketch with charcoal or chalk directly on the plate, or trace down over a chalky transfer paper. Remember that the plate is sensitive to any greasy materials (even fingerprints), so pencils or crayons cannot be used for guidelines not intended to appear in the final print.

You can apply the full range of drawing and painting techniques – line drawing with crayon, brush or pen, free liquid washes, sponged, spattered, and drybrushed textures. It is also possible to make erasures at this stage to correct any errors. When the plate is fully drawn up, the image is dried, dusted, and fixed; then it is covered with a layer of gum and must be left for a while, preferably overnight, before the next stage.

Sensitizing the plate
1 Hold the plate under running water and allow the whole surface to become fully wet. Drain off the excess water, but keep the plate damp.

2 Pour on the counter-etch solution and use a sponge to spread it evenly over the whole surface of the plate.

113

3 Hold the plate under running water and rinse off the solution thoroughly. Drain off the excess water.

4 Dry the surface of the plate completely. A hairdryer is valuable studio equipment, as the need to dry the plate quickly recurs throughout the lithographic process.

5 Sponge gum arabic around the edges of the plate to make a border for the image area. Allow the gum to dry.

Working study
The lithograph shown in the following demonstration is to print in only two colors, so the artist has prepared her idea of the image quite carefully beforehand in a sketch and more detailed color study (above). This gives her guidelines for the basic shapes in the composition, the balance of tones and the interaction of line work with broader areas of color. However, as the image is allowed to develop freely as the plates are prepared, the finished lithograph (see page 123) will be different in character and detail.

Drawing on the plate

1 If you wish to transfer the guidelines of a working drawing to the plate, you must use a non-greasy transfer paper so the lines will not appear after processing of the image.

2 Place your drawing over the transfer paper and work over it with a pencil or pen to press down the main lines of the image onto the plate.

3 Start to draw direct on the plate with a lithographic crayon or pencil. You can work exactly as you would with chalk or pencil on paper.

4 Apply the lithographic ink with paintbrushes, again working as you would on paper. You can use the ink at full strength or diluted with distilled or tap water.

5 You can apply ink with a sponge, as here, or with a rag or other applicator to vary the textures of your drawing. Here, paper masks are used to contain the sponging.

6 Continue until the image is completed in as much detail as you require. Keep in mind that this image will print uniformly as tones of one color.

First-stage processing
1 When all the ink drawing is completely dry, dust the plate with talc spread with clean absorbent cotton or a soft cloth.

3 Brush on the liquid-etch solution, covering the whole surface of the plate evenly and generously. This helps to "fix" the drawn image on the plate. Leave it on for just a couple of minutes.

4 Put the plate under running water and rinse off the etch solution thoroughly. Use the hairdryer to dry off the plate completely.

2 Repeat the dusting with powdered resin. These dry materials temporarily counteract the greasiness in the image, so it will accept

liquid processing in the next stage.

5 Sponge a thin layer of gum arabic over the whole plate surface and allow it to dry.

Leave the plate overnight before continuing the processing.

PROCESSING THE IMAGE

This stage is a second "etch" that strengthens the effect of the greasy marks on the plate surface. It is very similar to the preparatory stages, except that this time the drawn image is washed out and the marks are treated with asphaltum or printing ink. This makes the color appear different, but as you take out the original drawing and put color back in you have the opportunity to check how effectively the marks have set into the grain of the plate. This is where you begin to see the real appearance of the image for print and can judge how well the textures have developed. Again there is an opportunity for correction, using an erasing fluid.

When the image is satisfactory, it is rolled with ink as if for printing, gummed, and left to stand. The processing stages are repetitive, but as with any technical methods, you will soon become quicker and more expert in seeing them through.

Second-stage processing

1 Use mineral spirits and a clean rag to wash out the drawn image from the surface of the plate. All the black disappears, but you can still see the marks as a greasy "shadow" on the plate. The gum is unaffected by mineral spirits and continues to protect undrawn areas of the plate.

2 Rub in a thin layer of printing ink. This helps to reinforce the image and preserves delicate wash effects. Alternatively you can use asphaltum, which strengthens the textures and is better suited to a heavier, denser drawing.

3 Wipe out the ink with mineral spirits, then wash the plate with water to remove the gummed layer still surrounding the image.

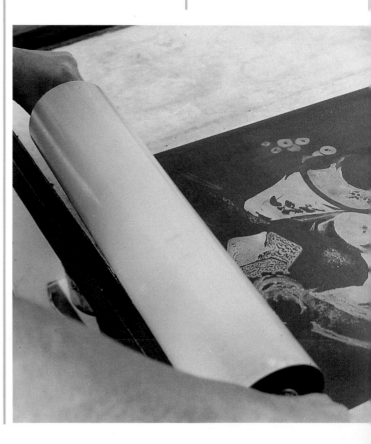

4 Roll up the damp plate with printing ink. The image now appears as it will print. Dry the plate and cover the surface with gum. Let it stand for at least half an hour.

PRINTING

This sequence demonstrates offset printing in two colors from metal plates. The basic techniques are the same for direct printing from stone or metal, except for the action of the press.

Generally, a litho plate is inked with a large, wide roller that covers the width of the image area in one pass, giving an even, consistent coverage of color. The difference between lithography and the other processes as far as printing is concerned is that the plate has to be wetted before any ink is applied and kept damp while it is rolled up. The water protects the clean, non-printing areas of the plate, but does not affect the ink's adherence to the greasy printing areas.

When the ink layer is dense and even enough to print, the plate must be dried off completely before paper and plate are positioned on the bed of the press. The mechanism of the press brings the thick rubber "blanket" of the roller into contact with the plate on the first pass, and on the way back the roller is pressed over the paper, transferring the inked image. It may take two or three passes to build up enough ink on the roller to print off clearly. You can then run your final prints.

When printing in two or more colors, the basic procedure for each one is the same, but you need to register them accurately on the previous printing. There are various ways of registering, but most presses are equipped with grippers and stops that enable you to position the paper correctly in relation to each plate. In this example, the second color is first printed on an acetate sheet attached to one end of the press. The print of the first color is positioned underneath the acetate, aligning the color areas. The stops are then set at the edges of the printing paper so that further prints can simply be slipped into place.

Offset printing
1 Mix a quantity of printing ink and roll it out evenly on a glass slab. Use a large roller that will cover the image area. The artist is working here with a gradated shade of pink; she has mixed three shades of the same color and rolled them out together.

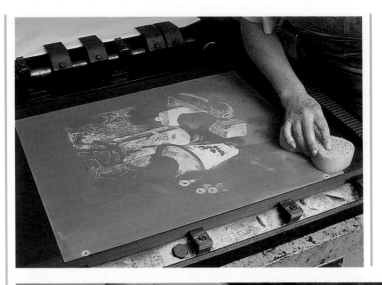

2 Use a wet sponge to remove the gum arabic from the plate. Position the plate on the bed of the offset press. Keep it damp throughout the rolling-up process.

3 Roll the color over the image area on the plate firmly and evenly. As necessary, wipe the surface with a damp sponge to remove any ink residue that may float on the non-printing surface.

4 When a sufficiently heavy and even color layer has adhered to the image, dry the plate completely. If it remains damp, moisture will be picked up on the press roller and spread onto the printing paper.

5 Roll the press roller back and forth over the inked plate until the image is clearly picked up on the roller "blanket" (the rubber covering). Mechanisms for these presses vary; at this stage the roller is not making contact with the area where the paper lies on the press bed.

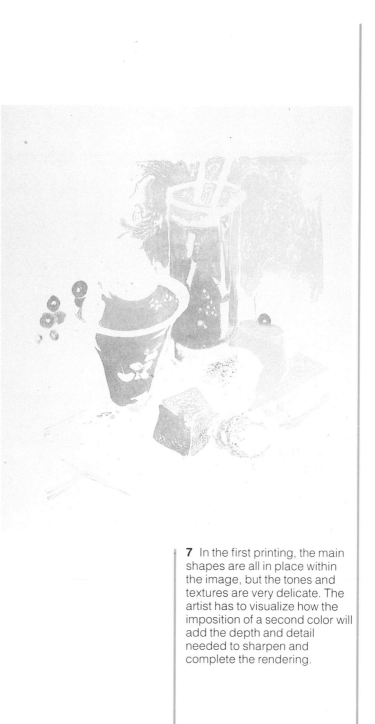

6 Position the paper on the bed of the press adjacent to the plate. The press has grippers to keep the paper flat and in place. Take the roller over the plate and back to pass over and make contact with the paper, laying down the inked image.

7 In the first printing, the main shapes are all in place within the image, but the tones and textures are very delicate. The artist has to visualize how the imposition of a second color will add the depth and detail needed to sharpen and complete the rendering.

Registering the second color
1 The artist has planned this print so that both colors are gradated, giving tonal variation across the whole image. She lays out the three mixed shades of the second color on the mixing slab.

3 The plate is put in place on the press and inked with blue. The first print is taken, by the same technique as previously, on a sheet of acetate anchored at one end of the press.

4 A print from the first plate is positioned under the acetate and moved until the image areas register exactly.

2 The large roller is used to work the ink evenly back and forth on the glass slab, until the three colors merge together smoothly.

5 Keeping the print in place, the artist adjusts the stops on the press that butt to the side and bottom edges of the printing paper. Methods of registering and marking the position of the paper may vary, depending on the press model.

6 The second color is printed onto each of the pink prints, each time positioning the paper against the fixed stops, and holding it in place with the grippers. As before, the roller is taken across the press over the plate, then back to lay down the blue image on the print.

7 In the final print, the strength of the shades of blue emphasizes particular shapes, as does the greater amount of linear drawing included in this image. But the two colors integrate convincingly to give the still life depth and form.

THEMES

❋

LEARNING TO USE A PRINTMAKING MEDIUM CREATIVELY IS A
TWO-STAGE PROCESS. FIRST, YOU HAVE TO FIND OUT WHAT
IT DOES; THEN YOU HAVE TO SEE HOW THAT POTENTIAL
APPLIES TO THE STYLE AND CONTENT OF YOUR WORK. ONE
WAY TO LEARN IS BY LOOKING AT FINISHED PRINTS AND
UNDERSTANDING HOW THEY HAVE BEEN CONSTRUCTED, IN
WHAT WAYS THEY EXPLOIT THE SPECIFIC PROPERTIES OF
THE MEDIUM OR EXTEND THEM INVENTIVELY. THIS GALLERY
SECTION EXHIBITS A VARIETY OF MEDIA, SUBJECT MATTER,
AND STYLES OF WORK, RELATED AS MUCH AS POSSIBLE
DIRECTLY TO THE TECHNIQUES ALREADY DESCRIBED.

LINE AND TONE

MONOCHROME PRINTS • LINE QUALITIES • SHADING AND LAYERING

Line is a particularly strong element of relief prints and certain intaglio processes, because of the basic techniques in these media and the physical character of the materials used. In monochrome linocuts and woodcuts, where lines form the boundaries of shapes and contribute pattern and detail to the rendering, line qualities are often relied upon to develop visual interest. The quality can vary according to the texture of the relief block – fine line work is difficult on coarse-grained wood or linoleum, for example. Such practical considerations need to be accommodated when you consider a style of work suited to the subject.

Drypoint is essentially a linear medium, and etching is said to have the most expressive and variable line qualities of all print media, because these derive both from your drawing skills and the action of the acid. However, you rarely see an etching that is completed in line only – more often the line work is combined with smooth aquatint tones and coarser textures created in a variety of ways.

All of these media also lend themselves to black-and-white renderings, from the strong graphic con-

trast of relief prints to the subtle shadings of aquatint. Since it is always technically possible to include color, a strictly monochromatic interpretation is the artist's deliberate choice. It can contribute a pleasing simplicity and directness, or a complex, layered, and textured effect, like a heavily worked drawing.

Monoprint and lithography are more painterly media, inviting you to exploit the effects of broad areas of tone and color. Pure line drawing is unusual in a monoprint, and it has to be done with a "broad brush" approach, but the example on this page shows how vigorous and colorful it can be, despite the economy of means. In lithography, the balance of line with mass and texture in a composition is largely a matter of the individual artist's style and the special features of the subject – all kinds of effects associated with crayon or pen drawing and watercolor painting can be achieved using a limited palette or full color range. Glorious color is one of the great pleasures of screenprinting, but this does not preclude the use of linear elements; and tonal balance is an important ingredient of making strong colors work effectively.

▶ **Anita Klein**
Swimming Lesson (drypoint)
The richly burred texture of drypoint provides a line quality that is both fluid and bold. The artist varies line thickness to emphasize the curving contours of the figures, which are deliberately stylized with a simplicity that is both elegant and playful.

◀ **Carole Katchen**
Embroidered Hat (monoprint)
The printed impression reflects the spontaneity of vigorous brush-drawn lines in this rendering. Their boldness is enhanced by the transition through subtle color variations that describe different parts of the figure. Open, irregular shapes created by the outline drawing are nicely offset by the repetitive detail of the pattern areas.

Caroline Bilson
St. Pancras Station (lithograph)
This print creates such a finely
varied impression of the
architectural detail in the
subject, it is surprising to
discover that the line work is
drawn freely and decisively
with the relatively coarse
medium of lithographic crayon.
To give full impact to the
intricate structure, the color is
confined to gentle washes of
diluted litho ink, using evenly
matched middle tones of warm
red and neutral gray. More
emphatic tonal variation occurs
where the washes are
combined with roughly shaded
crayon textures.
● Lithography: preparing the
plate, pages 113–117

St. Pancras Station 5/6 June, 1983   Caroline Bilson

Sally Robson
Chairs and Shadows (linocut)
Relief printing techniques lend themselves to strong monochrome imagery, interpreting the subject as a bold pattern of light and shade, often anchored, as here, by a firm, rhythmic line. The balance of this image comes from the varying directional forces of the lines, and the powerful graphic contrast of solid black and white shapes. The curving design draws attention to the more complex detail at the center of the image, where the positive shapes are counteracted by the heavy cast shadows.
● Linocut: cutting the block, page 30

▶ **David Carr**

Jerusalem (etching)

The tonal weight of this image comes from detailed line work, where hatched and crosshatched lines drawn in hard ground have been used to develop dark masses and interlocking forms. This is contrasted with open areas of white crossed by more fragile, sketchy lines and random marks that increase the textural variation. A light aquatint gives delicate shading to the background landscape.

● Etching: drawing on the plate, pages 90–91; aquatint, pages 94–95

Punta Sabbione   *Moira Wills '86*

◀ **Moira Wills**

Punta Sabbione (screenprint)

Despite the solid color areas, this screenprint is very linear in character, not only because of the fine lines cut for the black stencil. The narrow loop of the sea creates a strong directional curve, defined by color changes rather than a visible outline. The colors contribute a well-chosen tonal balance to the image, at the same time creating a fresh, descriptive impression of the sunlit bay.

● Screenprinting: hand-cut stencils, pages 62–67

> **Trevor Price**
> *Cyclamen* (etching)
> This is an aquatint using a technique that imitates the effects of the mezzotint process. The aquatint was laid over the whole plate and etched in acid to produce a very dark tone. The grays and whites were then brought out by burnishing down the aquatint texture to different degrees. This process enables the artist to create very subtle gradations of tone, particularly visible here in the soft folds of the fabric. However, the subject has also suggested a linear element, interpreted as white lines on black, in the vein patterns of the cyclamen leaves.
> ● Etching: aquatint, pages 94–95
> ● Mezzotint, pages 80–83

GRAPHIC IMPACT

LINE AND SHAPE • EDGE QUALITIES • CONTRAST

A picture that has strong graphic impact draws your attention immediately. There are certain elements of style and composition that practically guarantee this kind of instant attraction – calligraphic line, bold shapes, hard edges, powerful tonal contrast, bright color, repetitive pattern. All these are used to draw the eye to ephemeral graphic communications, such as posters and advertisements. The pitfall for the artist is that relying on these elements too simplistically can create an image that has impact, but reveals all in the first viewing. Ideally, a fine art print is something that can stand long or close acquaintance, so the initial impression contains additional subtleties to be discovered and appreciated.

What usually delivers this more lasting richness is a degree of variability, an unexpected touch. The relief printing media, especially woodcut and linocut, lend themselves to apparently simple, impactful approaches – clear-cut black-and-white images are typical of these processes and make naturally strong graphics. They need to contain beautiful or disturbing shapes; controlled but fluid line work; distinct edge qualities; crackling textures. Making use of a

medium's restrictions can sometimes be as effective as trying to extend its potential. The strictly practical advantages of monochrome block prints are that they are easy to produce and the materials are inexpensive.

The techniques of preparing and printing lithographs, screenprints, and etchings invite you to conceive images with a more complex amount of layering or surface activity. Of these media, screenprinting is most likely to be associated with strikingly graphic imagery; certain stencil processes encourage this quality, and the process has been widely used for printing posters. Lithography, too, has a direct association with posters and illustrations; its graphic qualities can combine with or supersede its more painterly effects. Pictorial impact can come from dynamic composition or vibrant color.

Etching is characteristically a more reticent and subtle medium, but because you can apply many different techniques to a single plate, all etchings have an underlying graphic unity that draws together the variations of line, shading, texture, and color. This makes an etched image all the more expressive, whether it is simple or complex.

◀ **Rebecca Owens**
Granada and 1850
(monoprint and linocut)
The bold graphic organization of the building's façade is defined by a cut linoleum block printed over color areas previously monoprinted from an uncut block. The artist also added light watercolor washes to knock back some of the stark white lines around the windows.

▲ **Carole Katchen**
Old Woman of the Andes
(woodcut)
The extreme contrast of black and white creates its strongest impact when the picture area is divided into simple, powerful shapes. Relief printing techniques encourage a bold approach to the balance of dark and light, but the artist has provided visual interest in the background by working with the wood grain to produce a halftone effect. There is a clever counterpoint in positive/negative interchange between the black lines mapping the old woman's face and the white lines on black describing the folds of her wrap, enhanced by sensitive line variation.

▼ Ian Mowforth

Dancing Figures (linocut)
Repetitive shapes create harmony and rhythm, but they are sufficiently varied to engage the viewer's attention in each section of the print, as well as making a lively overall design. The graphic black line forms the character of the image, nicely contrasted with more delicate textures and colors in the collaged papers underneath. The nine square blocks were cut separately, so they could be assembled in any order for printing.

▲ Paul Smith

Angry Christ (etching)
Intaglio techniques have been established for centuries, but new refinements can be found. This etching was made on Solarplate, which eliminates the use of acid. A positive, opaque image is exposed onto the pre-sensitized plate in sunlight (or artificial UV light) and washed out with water, which "etches" the design. Here the artist has used the new technique to produce a striking icon-like interpretation of a traditional subject.

◀ **Pip Carpenter**
Red Rocks of Danger
(lithograph)
Lithography allows the artist to create a striking, atmospheric image with bold brushstrokes and crayon drawing. The warm color range of the restricted palette reduces contrast, but the arrangement of shading introduces depth and distance without devaluing the strong graphic pattern of the black marks.

● Lithography: preparing the plate, pages 113–117

Colin Paynton
Loons (wood engraving)
The dramatic curves and rhythms of the overall composition create immediate impact, anchored by the solid black shapes and clean white lines. But the complex and inventive variations of stippled or hatched textures gradually draw the eye into many subtle layers of graphic detail.

▶ **Tiffany McNab**
Cheese Plant (etching)
Although the coloring of this etching is very subtle, the organization of shapes and balance of tone make it a particularly arresting image. The twisted stems and large leaves of the cheese plant draw the eye because they form a strong graphic pattern, emphasized by their dark color. Those bold, rather stark shapes make an interesting contrast with the regular, solid objects in the foreground and their intricate pattern detail.

◀ **Jonathan Heale**
Catnaps Edition (woodcut)
A simple, everyday subject becomes an unusual, witty composition when seen from an unexpected angle. By treating the human subject almost as a background element, the artist finds a strong combination of large and small shapes, and makes the most of the bright patterning that frames the simple, elegant form of the cat. The print is a black-and-white woodcut hand-colored with watercolor paint.

Paul Bartlett
Pretty Little Song Birds
(screenprint)
Rather than prepare separate images for each color, the artist used one screen and added to the painted stencil after each printing, gradually reducing the open areas of the screen mesh – a process similar to the reduction method of relief printing. The variety of coarse and subtle textures gains impact from the organization of related colors and contrasting tones.
● Screenprinting: filler stencils, pages 70–73
● Woodcut: color printing, pages 40–45

PATTERN AND TEXTURE

SURFACE VALUES • VARYING TONE AND TEXTURE • FORMAL PATTERNS

Many prints are executed in black and white or a restricted color range, which in turn restricts your use of color as a way of varying the surface qualities and making the shapes interactive. Certain media, particularly block prints, also preclude the subtleties of shading used conventionally to model form. Pattern and texture can perform both of these functions in a composition, so they are particularly important elements of printmaking.

Texture works in three distinct ways in prints; first, each medium has characteristic textural qualities to do with the materials and the kinds of marks that you can make

on or with them – one of the most easily identifiable examples is the slight graininess typical of lithographs, because the litho plate itself has a definite grain; there is a similar effect in the aquatint process in etching. You can also use different techniques to create textures intended to match or stand in for specific textures in the subject; or you can exploit similar processes simply to make the surface of the print more interesting.

Pattern is not inherent in printmaking materials, but in some cases the patterns you can easily make are directly related to the tools. The V-tools and gouges used in linocut and woodcut lend themselves to broadly hatched lines – straight, curving, or spiraled – and relatively coarse dot patterns or V-shaped, short cuts. A drypoint or etching needle is ideal for fine hatching and crosshatching, and also delicate stippling. Wood-engraving tools have a lighter touch than gouges, but cut more broadly than intaglio needles. Discreet patterns of lines and dots are a way of creating shading and gentle gradations of tone, and have been used as such in prints and drawings for centuries.

There is a crossover between pattern and texture in purely visual terms. The texture of foliage, for example, might be simulated by making a rough pattern of aquatint tones. Sometimes it is the overall feeling for shape and structure in the image that creates an impression of patterning, whether or not individual shapes contain surface variation.

▶ **Elisabeth Harden**
Goldfish (lithograph)
The translucency and
reflectiveness of the goldfish
pool is conveyed by preparing
the plate images with
lightweight crayon drawing and
washes of lithographic ink, then
printing with semi-transparent
layers of color. The cool, neutral
color range works equally
effectively in representing the
water and the stone statue.
Broad shading in warm yellow
suggests the denser textures of
flowers and foliage.

◀ **Roland Stringer**
Room 61 (wood engraving)
The delicate touch of the
engraving tools gives great
charm to printed textures in a
small-scale wood engraving.
Variations from coarse to fine
marks in hatched or stippled
areas transform black-and-
white contrast into a full tonal
range.

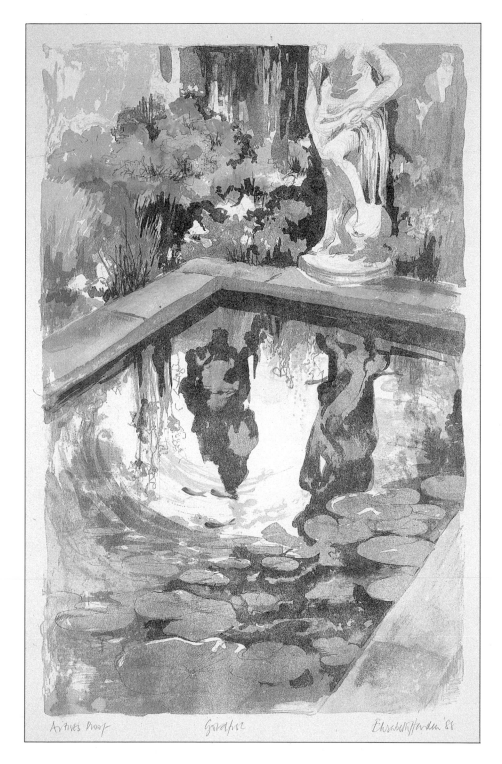

David Koster
Burnet Moth (lithograph)
There is a strong linear quality to this composition which creates both visual texture within the print and a sense of the natural textures in the subject. The artist draws in litho ink, using quill pens and brushes, to prepare the black plate, which forms the key design for additional color plates. The printing inks are made very transparent, to gain the maximum effect from overprinting. This also emphasizes the grain and fragile edge qualities of the washes. Occasionally, the artist adds touches of strong color by direct stenciling onto the   . finished print, where a small color area does not justify processing of another plate.

Richard Don Gabriel
Bathing Women (woodcut)
This image captures a lively sense of movement and interaction by concentrating each element of the subject into a formal pattern device. The balance of tones is beautifully organized by letting the white play a strong role in the mosaic and striped patterns representing the swirling water, while keeping the patterns of the women's clothing relatively dark so their bodies form graceful black silhouettes. On a close-grained wood block, the cut shapes remain crisp, and the ink prints with an even, dense texture.

Phil Greenwood
Meadow Clocks (etching)
In painting, the color interest of
a landscape subject often
dominates, drawing attention to
the broad impression rather
than the intricate detail. But the
natural textures of grass,
foliage, and flowers are ideal
for the scale and subtlety of
etching. The complex tracery of
linear drawing in the
foreground is sharpened by the
soft aquatint texture of the dark
trees, and this textural balance
is further developed by the
strong tonal pattern of the
image.
● Etching: drawing on the
plate, pages 90–91; aquatint,
pages 94–95

Paul Bartlett
The Empty Chair (etching)
The sugar-lift etching technique enabled the artist to make a detailed painting of the subject on zinc plate and reproduce the shapes positively. The plate had been coated with aquatint resin so the image would etch with subtle tonal variations and grainy texture. A striking, almost photographic, effect is achieved through the well-judged combination of meticulous, small-scale detail and boldly contrasted, broad areas of light and shadow.
● Etching: sugar-lift process, pages 98–99

Sonia Rollo
Ginger Jar and Anemones (etching)
In this charming still life, the natural pattern effect of curving flower stems is briefly echoed by the sparser, painted pattern on the jar. The colors are printed from three plates, so that different colors and textures overlap. The soft forms of leaves and flower petals were formed by impressing marks in a waxy soft ground.

The gentle aquatinted color gradations of the blue jar are created by the etching technique known as "spit-bite": rather than immersing the plate in acid, selected areas are dampened and a dilute acid solution dropped in. This allows controlled biting of soft-edged shapes.
● Etching: soft ground, pages 96–97

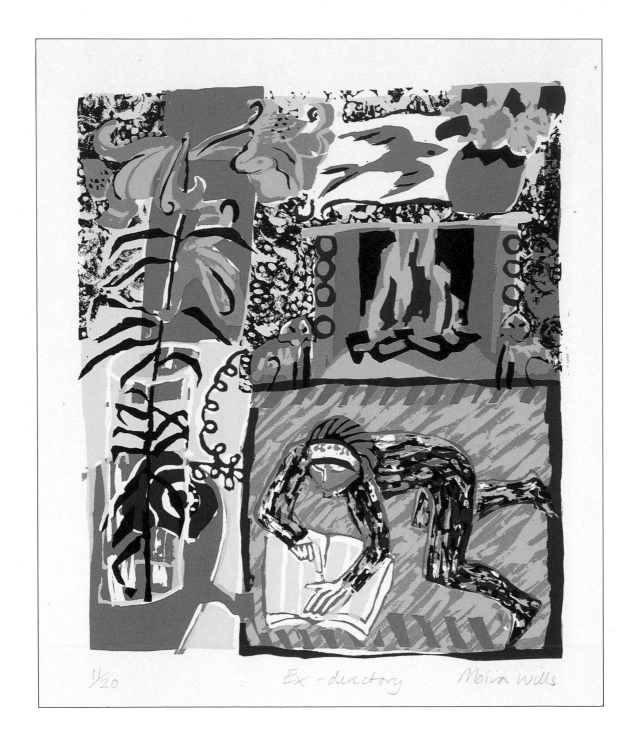

1/20   Ex - directory   Moira Wills

◀ Moira Wills

Ex-directory (screenprint)
The print's all-over textures, bold patterns, and brilliant colors match the vigor and spontaneity of a directly painted surface. Part of the fascination of the image is the way some shapes seem either to overlap randomly or not quite fit together, which adds to the energy. The hand-painted textures are active and occasionally unpredictable. It takes great confidence and discipline to achieve these effects so successfully in a print medium, where the final impact remains unknown until the last color is printed.

● Screenprinting: filler stencils, pages 70–73

▶ Rebecca Owens

Japanese Fish (monoprint and linocut)
This print successfully integrates a limited selection of strong colors, using pattern to enliven the stylized, simplified shapes. Broad color areas were put on paper by monoprinting, then the cut linoleum block was printed over them in red and dark green, using small rollers or a brush to apply the different colors to the block. The darker red in the fishes' patterning was applied by hand after printing.

▲ John Elliot

River Scene (collage print)
An interesting combination of techniques has been used to produce this unusual, textured effect. The line work was printed from a zinc plate made by a commercial printer from the artist's original drawing. The broader impressions of shading and color were overlaid from relief "blocks" of varying levels cut from mat board. Inking with soft oil pastels rather than printing inks provided the gentle, textural color gradations.

COLOR

ADDING COLOR • THE PRINTMAKER'S PALETTE • DESCRIPTIVE AND EXPRESSIVE COLOR

Color plays a variety of roles in printmaking, one of which is to add a purely decorative element to images that were planned to work successfully in black and white. Two simple ways of imposing color on a monochromatic design are hand-coloring with watercolor or gouache, or applying collage to the paper before or after printing. You maintain the advantage of being able to produce multiple, identical prints, but combined with the means of making each one an individual interpretation.

More frequently, color is not just decorative but descriptive, relating directly to the colors of the subject; or expressive, conveying something about the artist's response to the subject and sometimes forming a characteristic element of personal style. Most of the printmaking media can easily accommodate multicolored images – any restriction is imposed not by the materials available, but by the effort you want to put into developing the image. Screenprinting, for example, has a potentially infinite color range – you can pre-mix as on the painter's palette. But to combine many colors, even when mixtures are produced by overprinting, you have to repeat many times the real physical labor of preparing stencils, pulling prints, registering colors, and cleaning the screen mesh.

It can be difficult to plan many successive color layers, and the graphic qualities of a print may be lost if the color relationships are too complex and busy. You need the confidence to predict how the color combinations will appear after all the printing stages, and perhaps to adjust your expectations during processing. A limited palette is often the wisest choice because it is a controlled form of expression. Some artists enjoy printmaking precisely for this reason – they find working as imaginatively as possible within well-defined processing stages more sympathetic than the apparent freedom of direct painting techniques – which can leave the questions of how to start and when to stop too bewilderingly open-ended.

Color in intaglio printing is often more limited, muted, and subtle than in other media because of the inking and printing methods. Bright or strong hues may be introduced as local color or to create a mood, while line and shading form the structure of the image. There is typically more emphasis on tonality than on colorfulness, but the effects can be very richly textured.

▼ **Elisabeth Harden**
Making Marmalade (lithograph)
Although lithography can provide a wide, painterly palette of tones and colors, a restricted color range can be particularly effective because of the layering and textures that can be included in the image. In this print the colors are used as descriptive features of the subject, but also form a subtle, muted visual contrast, using the opposite orange/yellow and blue/purple sections of the color spectrum.
● Lithography: printing, pages 119–123

◄ **Pip Carpenter**
Three Pomegranates (etching)
A rich, descriptive color effect has been achieved by printing from two plates – one inked in blue, the other with gradations of crimson, red, orange, and yellow. In the lower part of the picture, the blue lines and aquatinting provide local color and tone; in the fruits and background, blue creates a dark undertone for the warm colors.

▲ **Trevor Price**
Gaucin (drypoint)
Printed in four colors from four separate plates, this image shows each color clearly and also soft mixtures where they merge and overlap. There is an intriguing interplay between the heavy tones where ink is retained in the scratched lines of the drypoint, and the faint drifts of color picked up from the plate surface.
● Intaglio printing: color printing, pages 108–109

14/150   *Fen Bridge*   Glynn Thomas

Glynn Thomas

Fen Bridge (etching)
Whereas other printmaking methods typically rely on overprinting to vary the colors, the simplest method for intaglio processes is to apply the required colors to different areas of the same plate, so the whole image is inked and printed in one sequence. This creates soft transitions from one color to another, and the drawing qualities tend to play the strongest role in defining the subject. But in this etching the colors and shading describe the space of the landscape view and its patterns of light and shadow.

● Intaglio printing: color printing, pages 108–109

▶ Pip Carpenter
Hyacinths (drypoint)
A subject which has a strong pattern of individual shapes as well as integral vivid hues can be equally effective interpreted in monochrome or color. The potential for hand-coloring black-and-white prints leaves the artist free to make choices about the final presentation. Here the sensitive lines and rich blacks of the drypoint drawing are enhanced by vibrant watercolor washes built to varying strengths.

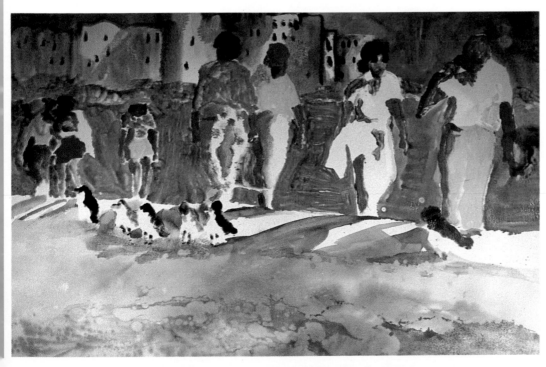

◀ June Ann Sullivan
Beach People (monoprint)
The image is prepared for printing using etching inks, with solvent to vary the textures. Where the ink is thickest, the colors are vivid and rich; together with broad white highlights where the paper is left bare, this creates the sunny mood of the picture. The foreground was added using transparent ink base with a touch of color.

Rebecca Owens
Summer Fruits (monoprint and linocut)
This lush, naturalistic color rendering was built up in three layers. Background color and undertones were first applied as a monoprint. The cut linoleum block describing the shapes and textures of the fruits was then inked in several colors, using small rollers and brushes to apply water-based block printing inks, and overprinted on the first color layer. Small touches intended to bring out the textural detail were added by hand, such as the opaque white highlights.

◄ **Edith Edwardson**
Royal Naval College (etching)
Deeply bitten areas of the
etching plate produce
characteristic broad, grainy
outlines, shadowy shapes, and
bold textures, giving depth to
the frontal view of the
architectural structure. The
unusual color combination
contributes a good effect of
tonal contrast, and the heavy
mauve-pink cast over the whole
image enhances the dramatic
portrayal.
● Etching: etched textures,
pages 100–101

► **Catherine Nicodemo**
*Seated Woman in her Dining
Room* (monoprint)
The melancholy mood of this
image relates directly to the
monochromatic palette. The
yellow is a somewhat acid
color, more so where it blends
into the grays and becomes
greenish. The dynamic contrast
of pure black and white shapes
subtly exaggerates the interior
space, in which the small figure
is almost an incidental detail.
The medium is heavily worked,
moist, watercolor paint.

▲ Ian Mowforth

Mackerel (linocut)
The simple, graphic shape and patterning of the fish is provided by the linoleum block. The glittering colors of the fish skin come from a collage of various materials – silver leaf, colored tissues, and printed papers. These were assembled on thin textured paper, which was then laid over the inked block to print the linocut. Because the paper is translucent, it was possible to see through it clearly to register the collage correctly over the black line work on the block.

● Linocut: proofing and printing, pages 31–33

Diana Croft
Rainbow Trout (lithograph)
The particular qualities of each printmaking medium assist the artist's interpretation of a subject. The shiny, scaly texture of the fish is a strong feature in this still life, as in the linocut opposite. Lithographic techniques enable the artist to build up shimmering color from delicate marks and textures – spattered ink and grainy crayon drawing. Red, yellow, and blue are strong colors, but they are cleverly merged and muted here with descriptive effect.

◀ **Sally Robson**
Royal Hill, Greenwich (etching)
Even when an image is mainly dependent on effects of line and shading for its descriptive qualities, color printing can add both visual interest and touches of local color. In this attractively "stacked" composition depicting closely built streets full of architectural detail, the subtle, warm colors create a more inviting mood than hard black, without detracting from the intricacy of the graphic interpretation.

COMPOSITION

FRAMING THE IMAGE • BALANCE AND RHYTHM • DIVIDING THE PICTURE PLANE

A printed image frequently requires more careful preliminary organization than a drawing or painting that can evolve freely on the working surface. The composition must relate effectively to the scale and proportions of the base material on which the image is prepared – particularly on a block or plate, because its edges usually show in the print. If part of the image is put down in the wrong place, or is out of proportion, it can be difficult to amend or erase it. If you are printing in more than one color, you need to be able to locate the colors accurately in separate printings, to register finally as a unified image.

You cannot tell exactly what you will see in a finished print until you print it, so many artists like to get a firm sense of composition through a working drawing or color study before beginning to work within the print process. The initial study may be used only as a reference guide or can be traced to form the basis of the print.

The elements of composition in printmaking are no different from those in any other artists' medium. The overall picture needs some kind of rhythm or

I'M HERE

balance – this can be mainly created by lines or by solid shapes and masses, with stresses running vertically and horizontally across the picture plane, diagonally or randomly. The image can be centralized and contained, or strongly related to the edges of the outer "frame." The shapes can be presented flatly, modeled with color and shading, or activated with patterns and textures. The spatial arrangement may be descriptive or formalized, recreating what is seen in the subject or interpreting your impression.

The variety of options you have depends both on the medium you are working in and the nature of your subject. None of the printmaking processes imposes absolute restrictions on the form of a composition, but you need to consider the character of your medium as you plan the image – the means of creating texture are, for example, less complex and subtle in linocut than in lithography. The pictures in this section are chosen to show how artists work inventively within the disciplines of their media, as well as demonstrating particular forms of pictorial organization.

◄ Kazumasa Nagai
I'm Here (screenprint)
The oval vignette is the dominant shape of this image, with the rectangular outer frame acting as a boundary to background color. The shapes of the creatures are elegantly fitted to the oval, but allowed to break through its shape just enough to disrupt the symmetry. Screenprinting offers particularly effective techniques for achieving powerful hard-edged shapes and clearly defined color areas.
● Screenprinting: hand-cut stencils, pages 62–67

Theresa Pateman
Spike of the Old Kent Road (linocut)
This witty linocut emphasizes the character of the dog by making him a massive, self-contained presence occupying more than half the picture area. This creates a very clean, strong division between the black and white shapes, although the strong linear detail conveys a sense of movement and interaction between different parts of the image.

June Ann Sullivan
Bikework III (monoprint)
A close-up view creates a rhythmic, abstract composition, but with many still-recognizable features that give the shapes a context. The original was painted in gouache on acrylic sheet and printed on damp, heavy watercolor paper. This provides the contrast between dense, bright colors and more fluid, wash-like textures. In choosing a water-based medium to work with, gouache was preferred to watercolor because its colors remain stronger after drying.

► **Glynn Thomas**
Pin Mill Window (etching)
A frame within a frame is an
interesting way of dividing the
picture surface formally. In this
case the window panes create
a very balanced, regular
division, but the view beyond
the window fills each rectangle
actively in a different way. The
informal curving and diagonal
lines of the boats' riggings play
against the fixed horizontal and
vertical framing.

Artists Proof   Pin Mill Window   Glynn Thomas

Judy Martin
Cheetah after Prey (etching)
One way of conveying a sequential element in the subject matter is to develop a series of images that can be printed together as one. This etching consists of three separately prepared plates assembled as a "triptych." Because intaglio plates are printed by direct contact and the image is reversed on the paper, the plates had to be positioned on the press in reverse order to obtain the correct sequence in the print.
● Intaglio printing, pages 102–109

▶ **Susie Perring**
Trick Cyclist (etchIng)
The spotlit "cyclist" is the center of attention at the physical center of the rectangle on which he is drawn. The shapes are simplified, but beautifully suggestive of mood and atmosphere, with active textures in the black areas that modify the harshness of such a strong tonal contrast. The rich velvety marks were formed by impressing a soft etching ground.
● Etching: soft ground, pages 96–97

Trick Cyclist — Susie Perring

◀ **Elisabeth Harden**
8 a.m. (lithograph)
In preparing lithographic plates, you have the same sensitivity of touch as in drawing or painting on paper. Crayon marks and washes can be gently faded out, to "lose" the edges of the image and disturb the effect of rectangular framing. It is possible to organize the balance of the composition so that printing on white paper makes the image appear as a completely free shape or, as here, loosely contained by a conventional format.

Colin Paynton
Puffins (wood engraving)
The hard end-grain blocks used in wood engraving enable the artist to control fine cutting techniques that create intricate texture. The halftone effect of stippling and hatching is beautifully balanced with solid areas of black and white. Every shape contributes to the rhythmic flow of the composition, which is both accentuated and counterpointed by the changing emphasis of the rippling lines.

● Wood engraving: cutting the block, pages 50–51

1/50   Katchen 1980

Carole Katchen
Yoruba Man (etching)
The figure makes a beautiful, fluid shape placed boldly at the center of the image area. An overly symmetrical sense of balance is avoided by the slant of his relaxed posture and the off-center shape of the table leading out of the frame in the foreground, which together make a diagonal pull through the image. The contrast of tonal shading and plain against patterned areas is perfectly judged.

► **Trevor Price**
Tiffany in the Bath (etching)
In a domestic interior, a view from above is unusual, and it introduces an element of abstraction. The clearly defined shapes divide the picture emphatically and isolate the pattern area on the right. The artist has also used the three-color printing to create spatial organization and modeling. The figure is described quite naturalistically, and a good pictorial solution has been found for the depth and movement of the bath water – by scraping back a dark-toned aquatint to retrieve pale shades. Some of the ripple pattern was also made by drawing in line through hard ground.
● Etching: applying hard ground, pages 88–89; drawing on the plate, pages 90–91; aquatint, pages 94–95; Intaglio printing: color printing, pages 108–109

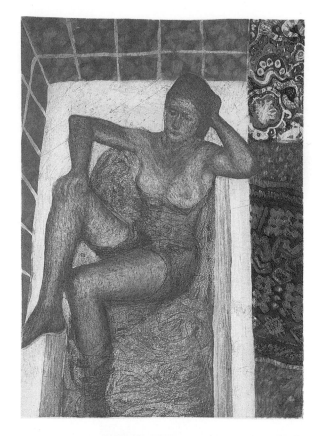

▼ **Sonia Rollo**
Checkmate (etching)
The checkerboard forms a regular grid on which the creatures are placed symmetrically, creating a mirror-image effect. The strong geometric balance works because the contrasts of light and dark tone, and of regular and organic shapes, provide visual interest across the whole surface.

Peter Strachan
Normandy Beach (screenprint)
The sky is often a significant
feature of an outdoor view, but
a very bold decision has been
made here in allowing it to
dominate the picture so
dramatically. The intensity of
the heavy, flat blue is offset by
the vivid handling of light
striking the white buildings on
the beach. This artist typically
uses hand-painted and
sometimes cut-paper stencils
combined with photographic
imagery. Special facilities are
required to prepare photo-
stencils and expose them on
the screen; photo techniques
can also be applied to etching
and litho plates.
● Screenprinting: hand-cut
stencils, pages 62–67; filler
stencils, pages 70–73

MOOD AND ATMOSPHERE

TONE AND COLOR • QUALITIES OF LIGHT • CREATING SPACE

Certain subjects are attractive because they convey a particular mood or sense of place which becomes an important factor in the artist's interpretation. Often this is best conveyed not by making a literal description of the subject, but by enhancing some quality within it that conveys the impression of mood and atmosphere.

Local colors – the colors that things really are – may be much modified by atmospheric effects or the pattern of light, especially in open landscape or in a shadowy interior. The typically restricted palette of a color print can be surprisingly effective in rendering these visual sensations. The artist can avoid distracting detail and focus on essential qualities of space, form, and light. This may mean organizing the variations of color, shading, and texture more rigorously than in a painting, where individual brushstrokes can deal with fleeting and subtle transitions. An image prepared for print must achieve a similar impact by more economical means.

The atmospherics of light are perhaps easiest to handle when there are distinct contrasts of light and shadow, especially in a medium that encourages

strong monochromatic interpretation, like etching or wood engraving. Dramatic contrast is interesting and needs careful management to achieve a coherent image without flattening the drama. Making light and space with color is a definite challenge, particularly where the image has a fairly balanced, even key in the light or medium range. Close relationships of hue and tone convey space and mood by subtle interactions – the detail and texture of the image play a significant role. A highly detailed drawing brings the viewer into the subject, whereas dissolving forms and contours open out the pictorial space.

Whatever your medium, the balance of shading and color is not immediately visible on the plate, block, or screen that you are working with. With experience, you learn more about the way the marks you make will translate into print, but the proofing stage of any print is always an exciting moment, when you see your idea take shape. The marks and the colors often remain open to adjustment until the final stages, enabling you to achieve images that are both precisely controlled and highly expressive, like the examples shown here.

2/200 Old Breakwater Joy Brand

Joy Brand
Old Breakwater (lithograph)
The gentle tones and textures that can be achieved with lithographic painting techniques enable the artist to produce a very delicate and subtle effect of light on water. The rendering is sparing of detail and effectively employs the limited palette to develop the spacious, atmospheric feeling of the view.
● Lithography: preparing the plate, pages 113–117; printing, pages 119–123

◀ **Donald Wilkinson**
Summer Window (etching)
Conventionally, etchings often begin with line work in hard ground and then progress to incorporating tone and texture, using the line drawing as a guide. This print, however, creates a gentle mood by eliminating hard lines and edges, using soft ground and aquatint techniques to achieve subtle shadings and ghostly forms. The tonal range provides a sense of space and modeling, but with low-key contrasts of tone and color.
● Etching: soft ground, pages 96–97; aquatint, pages 94–95

D. J. Carr
Captain Cook's Monument (etching)
This dramatic, silhouetted landscape view is darkly atmospheric, due to the tonal range and the varied marks of different etching techniques. The image was traced full size from a drawing and the main lines transferred to a plate coated with soft ground. The grainy line work so produced was developed with further drawing into hard ground, then the dark shading was applied with aquatint and the lights broadly "painted" by burnishing down the aquatint texture.
● Etching: drawing on the plate, pages 90–91; soft ground, pages 96–97, aquatint, pages 94–95

Donald Harris
Flurry (etching)
Rich, flat aquatint tones provide an atmospheric background to the whirling pattern of the birds and rippling water. The depth and mood of the image is enhanced by the color gradations and occasional strong contrasts. Two plates were overprinted to obtain this variety, one inked in blues passing from turquoise to violet; the other in yellow, orange, and red.
● Intaglio printing: color printing, pages 108–109

▶ **Glynn Thomas**
Kersey Garden (etching)
The yellow-green predominant in this charming composition gives a sunny, bright tone to the image, with the contrast of brown and dark green contributing space and depth. These colors were inked all together on the plate and printed in one: the brilliant red and yellow touches in the flowers were painted on the cleaned plate and overprinted.
● Intaglio printing: color printing, pages 108–109

Moira Wills
Papillon (screenprint)
Using medium to light-toned colors and an informal pattern of freely drawn shapes, the artist creates a bright, painterly image with much attractive detail and incident. It combines the small-scale fascination of plants and insects with the airy quality of open landscape and sky, without explicitly describing a particular location. The textures and edge qualities are cleverly varied by using a combination of stencil techniques.
● Screenprinting: hand-cut stencils, pages 62–67; filler stencils, pages 70–73

STYLE AND CONTENT

NARRATIVE • STYLISTIC INTERPRETATION • FORMALIZED IMAGES

Relief and intaglio printing have a long association with the traditions of graphic communication – woodcuts, for example, were one of the earliest forms of book illustration. These media readily lend themselves to subjects which seem to illustrate a storyline or contain a narrative of their own, in simple, direct images that "speak" to the viewer. Such subjects can be found in literary sources, in the incidents of everyday life, or in special events, representing particular or universal themes. Also in keeping with the narrative element, an artist may produce a series or suite of prints on one theme; the scale and detail of printed images provide suitable means of "publishing" information, commentary, and observation.

Apart from describing related events and images, a series of prints can also be unified by a distinctive style of imagery. There is a natural two-way stylistic development in the work of printmakers, who may choose a specific medium for its characteristic visual qualities, but also find that the techniques feed back ideas for appropriate forms of representation. The highly graphic qualities of prints, such as those described on pages 132–137, can encourage elements of personal style to become more strictly formalized than they usually appear within the looser disciplines of drawing and painting. For professional artists, a strong personal style is useful commercially; and they present themselves with the creative challenge of working out how that style can effectively interpret different elements of a theme, or widely differing subjects.

Printmaking techniques are an interesting area for artists working in a more abstract mode, in that the physical surface qualities of an image are specially important where the subject matter is less immediately accessible to the viewer. In this context also, strong graphic qualities are worth exploration; the materials and methods of the craft offer unique forms of interpretation that might not occur using other media and processes. But although abstraction tends to focus the viewer's attention on formal and expressive elements of composition, rather than recognizable forms, these purely visual properties are just as essential to the success of representational imagery, as can be seen throughout this gallery of prints.

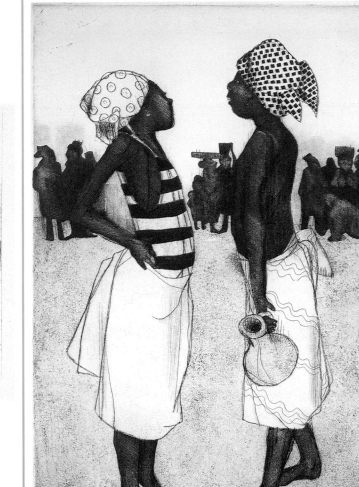

◀ **Mychael Barratt**
Animal Magic (etching)
The variety of surface effects achieved with the etching processes provides a full "vocabulary" of descriptive elements for figurative imagery. Soft ground and aquatint contribute rich, deep tones to the characterful drawing in this image, which is also hand-colored to enhance the strong graphic effect and highlight the main subjects.
● Etching: soft ground, pages 96–97; aquatint, pages 94–95

▲ **Elisabeth Harden**
South Downs Way (etching)
This picture tells a story in charming, cartoon-like style, relying on the economy and sensitivity of etched lines. It is full of incident, and the composition is cleverly organized to lead the eye through the image, taking in each event and the characters involved.
● Etching: drawing on the plate, pages 90–91

Carole Katchen
Daily News (etching)
The everyday occurrence makes a memorable image when the artist is alert to both the narrative and pictorial qualities. The postures of these Nigerian women precisely explain how absorbed they are in the gossip of the day. The figures are isolated in the foreground, but given a context with the formal pattern of background silhouettes. The tonal contrast is strongly emphasized, but both dark and light areas contain much subtle, active texture.

Kazumasa Nagai
I'm Here (screenprint)
This is one of a series of prints with a strong conservationist message (see also page 154), using the same basic structure to anchor the stylized representations of the creatures, which take on a powerful symbolic presence. The shapes, colors, and patterns are interpreted in a way that gives immediate graphic impact, each color printed from a separate screen to maintain the clarity of clean, flat shapes.

▲ Paul Bartlett
After Vincent (linocut)
There is a long tradition of
artists learning from or paying
homage to past masters by
reinterpreting their style and
imagery. In this linocut, the
direct, graphic qualities are
effectively employed to parallel
the heavy, swirling brushwork
of van Gogh's famous painting.
It is printed from one block by
the reduction method used for
both linoleum and woodcut
prints, re-cutting the design
after printing each color. The
ink has been rolled on thickly,
and overprinting produces
some interesting areas of
broken color.
● Woodcut: color printing,
pages 40–45

▶ Caroline Bilson
Brighton (linocut)
The recognizable architectural
features simplified into striking
patterns of black and white are
strongly representative of this
artist's style and express a
sense of place without going
into a literal description. Relief
printing media are ideal for this
kind of bold, dynamic image,
combining crisp contrast with
rough, aggressive texture.
● Linocut: cutting the block,
pages 30–31

◀ **Kristian Krokfors**
Roadside (screenprint)
The purely visual sensations of color play a dominant role in making an abstract image work. The color interactions are often complex and exact, which needs careful forethought when the printmaking process is planned. Although this interesting map-like composition has a harmonious, limited color scheme, it involved 15 separate screens, prepared with hand-cut drawn and painted stencils, to achieve the required variations of color and texture.

Sara Hayward
Purple Door (screenprinting)
This print is based on an interior scene, but uses shapes and colors abstractly to explore their emotive qualities and the moods created by color interactions. The screen stencils were prepared by drawing and painting with litho crayon and tusche, blocked in with gum arabic, and then washed out, so the applied marks print positively. The inks were mixed in different ways to achieve a contrast of translucent and opaque colors, in a palette selected to convey the personalized, expressive elements of the artist's interpretation.
● Screenprinting: tusche method, pages 74–75

INDEX

Page numbers in *italic* refer to captions

ACKNOWLEDGMENTS

Quarto would like to thank the following for all their help with this project:

The Print Gallery; CCA Galleries; and John and Shelia Elliot in the USA who researched many of the American examples in this book.

Tools and equipment featured throughout were kindly lent by T.N. Lawrence and Son (London and Sussex); L. Cornelissen and Son Ltd (London); George Hall (Sales) Ltd (London).

The following artists helped with the step-by-step sequences in the techniques section:
monoprint: Moira Wills, Judy Martin; linocut: Ian Mowforth, Moira Wills; woodcut: Caroline Bilson; wood engraving: Roland Stringer; collage prints: Judy Martin; screenprinting: Moira Wills; drypoint: Judy Martin; etching: Elisabeth Harden; lithography: Elisabeth Harden.

p10 Elisabeth Harden; **p11** Moira Wills; **p12** Collage print: Judy Martin; Etching: Elisabeth Harden; Wood engraving: Roland Stringer; Mezzotint: Phillip Coombs; Monoprint: Judy Martin; **p13** Woodcut: Caroline Bilson; Drypoint: Juliet Kac; Lithography: Elisabeth Harden; Linocut: Ian Mowforth; Screenprint: Moira Wills; **p83** Phillip Coombs; **p109** *top* Phillip Coombs; **p109** *bottom* Judy Martin; **p126** Carole Katchen; **p127** Anita Klein/Greenwich Printmakers; **p128** Caroline Bilson; **p129** Sally Robson/Greenwich Printmakers; **p130** *top* David Carr; **p130** *bottom* Moira Wills; **p131** Trevor Price; **p132** Rebecca Owens; **p133** Carole Katchen; **p134** *left* Ian Mowforth; **p134** *right* Paul Francis Smith; **p135** *top* Colin Paynton/Wildlife Art Agency; **p135** *bottom* Pip Carpenter/Greenwich Printmakers; **p136** *top* Tiffany McNab/Greenwich Printmakers; **p136** *bottom* Jonathan Heale; **p137** Paul Bartlett; **p138** Roland Stringer; **p139** Elisabeth Harden; **p140** David Koster/Wildlife Art Agency; **p141** Richard Don Gabriel; **p142** Phil Greenwood/CCA Galleries; **p143** *left* Paul Bartlett; **p143** *right* Sonia Rollo/Greenwich Printmakers; **p144** Moira Wills; **p145** *top* John Elliot; **p145** *bottom* Rebecca Owens; **p146** Pip Carpenter/Greenwich Printmakers; **p147** *left* Trevor Price; **p147** *right* Elisabeth Harden; **p148** Glynn Thomas; **p149** *top* Pip Carpenter/ Greenwich Printmakers; **p149** *bottom* June Ann Sullivan; **p150** Rebecca Owens; **p151** *top* Edith Edwardson/Greenwich Printmakers; **p151** *bottom* Catherine Nicodemo; **p152** *top* Ian Mowforth; **p152** *bottom* Sally Robson/Greenwich Printmakers; **p153** Diana Croft/Greenwich Printmakers; **p154** Kazumasa Nagai; **p155** *top* Theresa Pateman/Greenwich Printmakers; **p155** *bottom* June Ann Sullivan; **p156** *top* Judy Martin; **p156** *bottom* Glynn Thomas; **p157** *top* Susie Perring/Greenwich Printmakers; **p157** *bottom* Elisabeth Harden; **p158** Colin Paynton/Wildlife Art Agency; **p159** Carole Katchen; **p160** *top* Trevor Price; **p160** *bottom* Sonia Rollo/Greenwich Printmakers; **p161** Peter Strachan/Greenwich Printmakers; **p162** Donald Wilkinson/CCA Galleries; **p163** *top* Joy Brand/CCA Galleries; **p163** *bottom* David Carr; **p164** *left* Donald Harris/Greenwich Printmakers; **p164** *right* Glynn Thomas; **p165** Moira Wills; **p166** Mychael Barratt; **p167** *left* Elisabeth Harden; **p167** *right* Carole Katchen; **p168** Kazumasa Nagai; **p169** *top* Paul Bartlett; **p169** *bottom* Caroline Bilson; **p170** Kristian Krokfors/Pratt Contemporary Art; **p171** Sara Hayward.

Jacket images kindly supplied by Paul Bartlett, Mychael Barratt, Elisabeth Harden, Glynn Thomas, Moira Wills.